The Organized Student:
Teaching Time Management

by Claudia Vurnakes

illustrated by Tony Waters

FS-10168 The Organized Student: Teaching Time Management
All rights reserved–Printed in the U.S.A.
Copyright © 1995 Frank Schaffer Publications, Inc.
23740 Hawthorne Blvd.
Torrance, CA 90505

Table of Contents

Introduction

Along about April each year, teachers and students alike begin dreaming of the endless summer. September finds us all scratching our heads and saying, "Where did the time go?"

Where does time go? In today's fast-paced culture, we all have more to do and less time in which to do it. With the decline in traditional sources of other learning—home, church, youth organization— our schools have had to shoulder more and more responsibilities. We push ourselves and our students hard to cover all the bases every day, every year.

By middle school, most students are mature enough to understand the passage of time and its consequences. But they often lack the skills to manage and control their time. The results are like watching the proverbial frog in hot water. Some students do not realize they have landed in the pot. Others are so focused on completing day-to-day tasks, they do not feel the pressure heating to the boiling point. Experts agree, the best time for students to learn about time management is before their time becomes totally unmanageable.

This is the aim of this book. The teacher suggestions and reproducibles provided here will help your students take a good look at the importance of time management in their academic work, at home, and in their adult lives as well. The material is designed for flexibility, so you can work it into existing plans or pull out entire chapters to use as independent units. Early in the school year, focus on effective note-taking and ways to keep up with daily assignments. Offer a concentrated unit on getting organized when you assign lengthy reports or projects. Select activities on motivation throughout the year as needed.

Because many middle and upper grade students need a break from paper-and-pencil activities, this book includes games, teaching bulletin board ideas, cooperative and independent learning assignments, skits, simple art activities, even an occasional story or poem to read aloud. Each chapter opens with a poster for your room. Enlarge on a copier, add color, and laminate for some humorous views of student dis-organization!

As the world rushes down the "information superhighway," we know that many of the facts we teach today will be obsolete tomorrow. But if we can teach our students how to get organized and how to put their time to the best use, we will have equipped them well for whatever the future holds.

chapter
1

Chaos: Facing the Problem

Keeping Pace

The impression that life speeds up the older we get is universal. For the first time, middle-schoolers are faced with adjusting to a faster pace. Trouble results when their internal clocks are still at a slower setting, and they find themselves falling further and further behind. Examine the problem with a chart that focuses on the various aspects of a student's life. Suggested responses appear in the blocks below; students' actual answers will vary.

How the Pace of My Life Has Changed

	Lower Grades	Now
Learning New Skills	Lots of time to listen and learn. Teacher went over things again.	Teacher explains one time. If you miss it, you are out of luck.
Rest, Bedtime	Went to bed early. Often stayed awake thinking. Woke up fresh every day.	No time to daydream. Go to bed whenever work is finished. Always tired.
Playing, Relaxation	Went outside every day. Had free choice of fun activity when through with work.	Even P.E. is work! Only 30-minute lunch for relaxing.
Chores Required at Home	Made bed every day.	Make bed, mow lawn, vacuum room, walk dog, take out trash, do laundry, dust.

Temperature Rising

Even if you are indoors, you know it is hot outside when you see the mercury climb in a thermometer. How convenient it would be if human beings came equipped with a similar gauge, some visual indicator that would signal building pressure due to excessive busyness!

Help your students recognize their personal boiling points with this graphing activity. Draw a large thermometer on the chalkboard and create with the class a list of activities in a student's typical busy day. Next, shade in the thermometer to indicate those times the student felt rushed or too busy, deepening the shade to show an increase in pressure.

Woke up late.
Gulped breakfast.
Missed bus.
Barely got to school on time.
English class.
P. E. - rushed to change.
Science class.
Math class.
Lunch - worked on Spanish.
Spanish class.
Social studies class.
Soccer practice.
Got home late.
Ate leftover dinner.
Washed dishes.
Went shopping.
Took out garbage.
Started homework.
Had three phone calls.
Put homework away until morning.
Went to bed exhausted.

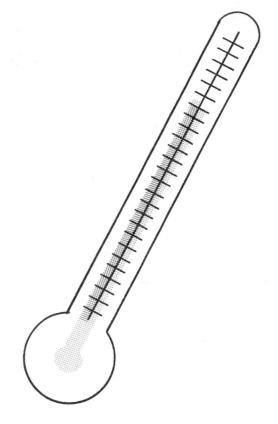

Provide students with long strips of paper, such as adding machine tape, so they can graph their own busy days. The purpose of this activity is two-fold—first, to show both you and your students the incredible number of activities that fill many students' days; and second, to recall the discomfort of those "too-busy" feelings and to resolve to deal with them.

Endless Orbit

Read the paragraph below to your students:

Sherrie sits down after dinner and starts her English assignment. As she opens her cluttered notebook, the basketball schedule falls out. Sherrie jumps up and phones her friend Trish to make plans to attend Friday's game. Just as Sherrie is about to hang up and get back to her English, Trish asks a question about math. The two girls spend the next 45 minutes trying to figure out an algebra problem, along with trading gossip. When she is finally ready to get back to English, Sherrie cannot find her worksheet.

Point out that the girl in this situation is easily distracted. Why is it that so many interesting things capture our attention the very minute we sit down to study? Many students find themselves flitting from one thing to another, forgetting the task at hand. They are trapped in an endless orbit just like Sherrie.

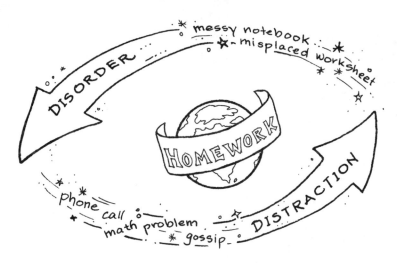

When we are disorganized, distractions lure us away from our job. This results in even more disorganization, with room for an ever-increasing number of distractions. So around and around we go, always trying, but never succeeding.

Direct students to write paragraphs describing their own endless orbits.

The Mystery of the Missing Notebook

If anyone can misplace a notebook, it's Professor Plum or Mrs. Peacock! To focus attention on how disorder at home affects the school day, assign the creation of original board games similar to Parker Brothers' Clue.

Students work in groups of four to create a gameboard that features rooms where school materials could easily be misplaced. Next, they make up three stacks of solution cards, one stack listing the different rooms, a second stack giving possible reasons for losing the notes, and a third stack listing suspects involved.

To begin play, a dealer selects one card from each stack to place face down on the gameboard. The remaining cards are shuffled and dealt. The four players take turns rolling the dice and traveling to a room where each can make a guess as to room, reason, and suspect. If another player holds any of the cards guessed, he/she reveals one of them, invalidating the guess. Play continues until all possibilities have been eliminated except for those cards placed face down on the board.

Creating and playing the game is challenging, and it helps students see the chaos connection between school and home.

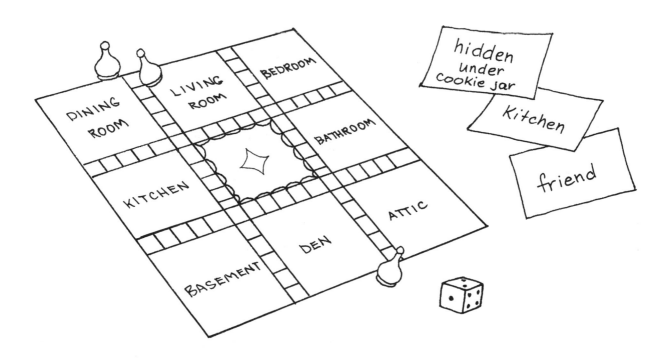

The Disorder Disorder

Aside from the price paid in poor grades and missed due dates, many students also pay emotionally when they are disorganized. How can a student tell if he or she has poor self-esteem due to a lack of order? Give your class the questions below. Allow some thinking time, then come together to discuss.

➤ How would you feel if your friends had to move piles of dirty clothes to find a spot to sit down in your room?

➤ How do you feel when your terrific ideas flop because you just do not have enough time to carry them out?

➤ How does it feel when you plan your work and complete a big project on time?

➤ How does it feel when your family has to rush to get somewhere, leaving family business half-done or skipped all together?

➤ Does taking care of "little things" (getting enough notebook paper, sharpening pencils) make for a better school day?

➤ How do you feel on a day when you oversleep and have to rush to get to school? Does oversleeping affect the entire day?

➤ Do you ever feel that if you were somehow a better, smarter person, you could handle your life much better?

Full of Hot Air

If there is one thing at which many students excel, it is making excuses. "I do not have enough time to get organized." "Being organized is too much work. I do not have that kind of energy." Excuses like these are full of hot air—the very time and energy people use inventing the excuses could be spent getting organized!

Sometimes the smallest, silliest excuses stand in the way of our success. "Every time I get my notebook organized, it pops open and all my papers fall out." "American students are not as good in math as kids from other countries."

Help your class examine the all-too-common habit of excuse-making with this hands-on activity. Direct students to write their favorite excuses on small strips of paper. Next, roll up the strips and insert them in balloons before inflating. Students then choose a balloon other than their own, pop it, and examine the reasoning—faulty or otherwise—of the excuse found inside.

Here are some examples to get you started:

➤ "I cannot get organized because my sister and I have to share a desk."

➤ "My grades are OK now, so I do not really need to think about time management skills."

➤ "I am not really worth it."

➤ "As soon as basketball season is over, I will have time to get organized."

➤ "Anyway, I am not going to college, so I do not have to worry about organizing my life."

Scientific Reasoning

Where does disorder come from? Why does it exist? Modern physics offers a scientific explanation. That state of utter confusion that we know all too well is the result of *entropy*, the disintegration of matter and energy to an ultimate state of idle uniformity. In other words, anything left to itself will break down, fall apart, or become disorganized.

Discuss this concept with your students and how it applies to these situations:
- a tree stops growing. (It gradually begins to decay.)
- a metal wheel stops turning. (It rusts in place.)
- a human being stops moving a muscle. (He or she wastes away and becomes useless.)

Does entropy apply to lockers, notebooks, science projects, bedrooms, careers, brains? Yes! Everything that exists on this planet is subject to the law of degradation. But knowledge is the beginning of wisdom. The very definition of entropy includes a clue to its resolution—"left to itself." When students face the fact that all of nature— including people—tends toward disorder, they begin to understand the need to take action. None of us can afford to leave well enough alone. Fighting chaos is a daily battle.

Student Reproducibles—Chapter One

The Chaos Quotient—Answers will vary. Many students do not recognize the symptoms of disorder. Use this activity for some self-evaluation. Follow up with a writing assignment. "I know I'm suffering from disorganization when...."

Whose Mess Is This?—Answers: A) Pile-It-On Paul, B) Pack Rat Patti, C) Laid-Back Larry, D) Contrary Mary, E) Choosy Charlie, F) Perfect Pamela. Assign students the task of writing a brief monologue for the character most like themselves. Students may create new characters if none of these fit.

Famous Last Words—Answers: 1. I, 2. B, 3. P, 4. P, 5. I, 6. I. Use this activity as the basis for some impromptu skits. Small groups of students act out other historical situations, working one of the frustrations from the reproducible into their dialogue. The class tries to identify the problem and the characters involved.

Name_____

The Chaos Quotient

Rating the Situation

Place a check mark by the statements that apply to you.

_____ 1. Completing homework assignments is a problem because I just cannot remember what I am supposed to do.

_____ 2. My friends would rather eat a stale garlic sandwich than open my locker.

_____ 3. I have to pull an all-nighter—two nights in a row—to get my science fair project finished on time.

_____ 4. Piano lessons, soccer practice, club meetings, orthodontist appointments, shopping trips, chores—who has time for homework?

_____ 5. By the time I find a pencil to borrow, the quiz is over.

_____ 6. Now, where did I write those science notes? Oh yes, they are on the back of last month's lunch menu.

_____ 7. I was absent and missed some assignments. Now I am so far behind, why bother?

_____ 8. I would like to study for the test, but my notes look like they were written in some kind of intergalactic code!

_____ 9. I was late for school this morning because I could not find the shoes I kicked under the sofa last night while I watched TV.

If you checked—

0-3   You are fairly well-organized. Keep up the good work!

4-6   Watch out! You are skating on thin ice. Your life could spin out of control at any time.

7-9   Call 911! Send out the cavalry! You are drowning in disorder, but take heart—by learning time-management skills you too can conquer chaos!

Whose Mess Is This?

Types of Disorganized Students

PART A

Being disorganized has nothing to do with being smart. Some of the smartest people in the world started out as disorganized students. These creative, intelligent people had attitudes that kept them from accomplishing those tasks they set for themselves. But when they replaced wrong ideas and habits with organized ones, the world took notice.

Look at the individuals below. See if you can match each one with the correct description. Then take a long look at your own ideas and habits. Are any of these attitudes standing in the way of getting *your* act together?

Pack Rat Patti

Choosy Charlie

Perfect Pamela

Contrary Mary

Laid-Back Larry

Pile-It-On Paul

Whose Mess Is This?

Types of Disorganized Students

PART B

A. This disorganized student never discards anything. Instead, he/she keeps stacking it up until there is just enough room to walk from the door to the bed. No matter how high the piles of clutter get, this student insists, "Yes, it is messy, but I know where everything is. That's all that counts, right?"

B. This disorganized student also never discards anything. He/she keeps every notebook, every old test, every almost-empty pen because "you never know when you might need it again." The question is, when that time finally comes, will this person be able to find that old set of notes?

C. This disorganized person takes a relaxed approach to life. He/she believes that being organized is just too much work. The sad truth is, disorganization creates much more work for this person in the long run. Having to redo lost or incorrect assignments does not make for an easy life.

D. This disorganized student is rebellious. He/she does the opposite of what is assigned just to show the teacher who is in control. Give this student directions and he/she looks for a different way to go. When the teacher asks for a report, he/she turns in a poem. Independent? Yes. Creative? Certainly. Capable of following instructions to the letter? No. And he/she pays a high price for refusing to get organized.

E. This disorganized student looks down his/her nose at ordinary schoolwork. What does keeping a neat notebook have to do with real life? He/she will get down to work when a truly *important* assignment is given. The trouble is, when it does, this student cannot handle it because he/she has not had any practice on the smaller tasks.

F. This disorganized student tries to live by the rule "Anything worth doing is worth doing right." He/she spends an incredible amount of time doing one assignment perfectly. By the time it is finished, this student is so exhausted that he/she rushes willy-nilly through the rest of the work. Overall performance: C-.

Famous Last Words

Common Frustrations

Being disorganized causes many people to quit long before they ever achieve any success. What makes you want to quit?

Think how different life would be if the people below had quit before they ever got organized. Read each statement below and diagnose the problem:

I = Impatient, quits at the first difficulty
P = Perfectionist, quits in disgust for being merely human
B = Big plans to change the world, but never gets the small jobs done

_____ 1. Abraham Lincoln: Is it fourscore and six years, or fourscore and seven? Bother, I never can remember those dates. Oh well, I will just skip that speech at Gettysburg. Who cares?

_____ 2. Julius Caesar: First I will conquer Germany, then France, then England. And I have heard of a land on the other side of the ocean.... What? You say my best friends are plotting to murder me? Do not bother me with such a little detail. I am off to rule the world!

_____ 3. Helen Keller: It is no use. If I cannot read Braille right the first time, I just will not read it at all.

_____ 4. Simón Bolivar: I quit! I have not persuaded all the people to join our revolt. What ever made me think I could help Venezuela win its freedom from Spain?

_____ 5. Sacajawea: Forget it, Lewis. I have looked for that ocean for an hour now. It just is not there. Clark and I are turning back.

_____ 6. Michelangelo: Stretch out on my back to paint a church ceiling? Impossible! This job is simply too difficult.

Choosing to Get Organized

Words to Live By

Language often provides clues about a society's values. Word-watchers know that the number of terms for an idea indicates its significance. That is indeed the case with the concepts of *superiority* and *mediocrity*. How many synonyms or expressions can students list for each category? Why are there so many words expressing *excellence*? Why don't we have as many terms for the idea of *second-rate*?

Many students never tackle the challenge of getting organized because they have talked themselves into settling for second-best. Which set of words would your students rather live by? Let's get organized and give people something terrific to talk about—us!

Superiority—*great, excellent, supreme, maximum, apex, victorious, crowning, champion, fabulous, peak, summit, superb, beyond wildest dreams, proficient, gifted, expert, ingenious, finesse, panache, masterful, triumphant, flying colors, knock 'em dead, smash hit, outstanding*

Mediocrity—*ordinary, so-so, commonplace, tolerable, fair, run-of-the-mill, vanilla, plain jane, passable, average*

Tru-Vu Goggles

What do you do when you have trouble seeing yourself clearly? You get a prescription for Tru-Vu Goggles! Here's a fun way to drive home the point that we all need to examine ourselves with honesty and clarity. Do we see ourselves realistically, as we truly are? Or do we suffer from inflated or depressed views of ourselves?

To make Tru-Vu Goggles with your class, cut apart the sections of a cardboard egg carton, leaving the cups connected in pairs. Pass out scissors, pipe cleaners, colored cellophane, and tape. Students cut viewing holes in the bottom of each cup and tape cellophane over the holes. Using pipe cleaners for the goggle stems, students don the goggles to write clear-eyed assessments of themselves and their need for time management principles.

If Only . . .

"If only I had started my project earlier...."
"If only I had made that shot...."
"If only I had not fallen asleep during class...."
"If only I had not made that choice...."

Have you ever played "If Only?" This mind game is extremely popular with people of all ages. But its wide appeal is difficult to understand, for it is a game of regrets only, and no rewards. People find themselves trapped in the game forever, never achieving, never enjoying the accomplishments life has to offer.

Teach your class a new game to play called "Next Time." Direct students to write their most frequent "if only" thoughts on paper. Then cross out the "if onlys," replacing each phrase with the words "next time." Students rewrite their statements to show how past failures can be steps toward future success.

The Tale of the F. A. I. L. Trap

The short story that follows shows that we each have a choice when we experience failure—to give up or to pull ourselves together and go on. There are several ways to use this story with your students. Simply read it aloud in class, ask an expressive reader to tape it for you, or assign parts and use the story as the basis for a drama, complete with sound effects.

In presenting the story, pause at the last two paragraphs and ask students to suggest possible endings. Afterwards, discuss Jamal's future. What happens next? Will Jamal ever land in the F. A. I. L. trap again? Will things be different? How does the worm use exaggeration as a weapon?

If your students enjoy this story, encourage them to write their own symbolic tales about perseverance and choosing to take control of their feeling of failure.

The Tale of the F. A. I. L Trap

Jamal looked at the bold red letter written across the top of his social studies report—F. Suddenly the floor gave way, and Jamal felt himself falling. For several seconds, cold, empty air whistled by his ears. Then Jamal landed with a thud on a hard dirt surface.

As soon as his head stopped swimming, Jamal looked around. There were dirt walls on all four sides. The only light came from a kid-sized hole in the ceiling overhead, which was made of branches loosely woven together. Shifting his feet, Jamal stepped on what he first thought was a stick. A second glance told him it was not a stick.

"B-O-N-E-S!" Jamal shrieked. "Where AM I?"

"Welcome to my humble abode." The voice was small and sinister. It was close—much too close—to Jamal's ear.

Whirling around to the opposite wall, Jamal looked straight into the eye of a huge worm curled on a ledge of dirt and roots. For a long moment, boy and worm glared at each other.

"Wha-what did you say this place was?" Jamal finally asked.

"I call it home," the worm said. "But it does have a name. Read for yourself." The worm gestured to a section of the wall.

In the filtered light, Jamal could barely make out some letters scratched in the packed dirt. "The F. A. I. L. Trap," he read out loud. "Those initials, what do they mean?"

"Let me see if I can recall. Oh, yes. Really, it's too simple," the worm said with a bored sigh. "F. A. I. L. stands for Feeling All Is Lost. Which of course, I never do."

Jamal looked puzzled.

The worm yawned. "Do I have to explain everything? Are all humans so . . . dense? All right, all right. Think back to what you were doing right before you landed here. What happened?"

"I was in social studies class, and the teacher was handing back our reports," Jamal said.

"Go on," the worm urged.

'Well, I saw an F on my paper, and . . . that's all I remember."

"How interesting," the worm said. "A case of Instant Surrender. I haven't had one like this in years. It usually takes several mistakes for people to give up all hope. Tisk, tisk, young man. You make dinner too easy. One F and down you come, right into my handy F. A. I. L. Trap. But where's the salt and pepper? All this idle chatter makes me hungry!"

Jamal gulped. "You mean . . . you're going to . . . to eat me?"

The worm smiled and looked at the bones littering the floor of the pit. "Do calm down, my boy. Agitation spoils a meal. After all, you've hit rock bottom. You're a disaster, a failure, a washout. You've blown it, totally and forever. You made an F on a social studies report, so you'll never amount to anything. That's what got you here, right, Feeling All Is Lost? You'll never get out of this pit alive."

Jamal's heart started pounding and the blood rushed to his brain. "You're right," he shouted at the worm. "I *did* feel that way when I saw an F on my paper. I wanted to give up, and I felt like I'd never be good at anything. But I just remembered something my teacher told me a long time ago. The only *real* failure is the one that does not teach you anything. Well, I've learned plenty today! I've learned how easy it is to wind up in this pit with no way out. I've learned that Feeling All Is Lost is a deadly trap. That's an important lesson, and I'm *not* a total failure. Move off that ledge, you disgusting old worm. I've got a social studies grade to work on, so I'm outta here!"

With a wild swoop, Jamal knocked the worm to the floor and pulled himself up to the ledge. One more heave and he was free. Down in the pit, the worm dusted himself off and tightened his belt. "Every once in a while, one gets smart," he muttered to himself. "Oh, well, I do need to lose a few pounds. It won't be long before another silly human condemns himself to the F. A. I. L. trap. Then I will get my feast."

Storm Watch

Meteorologists track the path of storms to learn weather patterns and prepare for the future. The same approach can work with patterns of human behavior. Show students how the problem of time mismanagement can grow into a storm of life-altering proportions.

Post a simple funnel-shaped spiral on a bulletin board. Label the base of the storm "Time Mismanagement." Next, distribute consequence cards and direct students to place them in correct sequence on the storm. What other outcomes can students add to the funnel? Follow up with this writing assignment: Create a fictitious character who experiences first-hand the storm of poor time management.

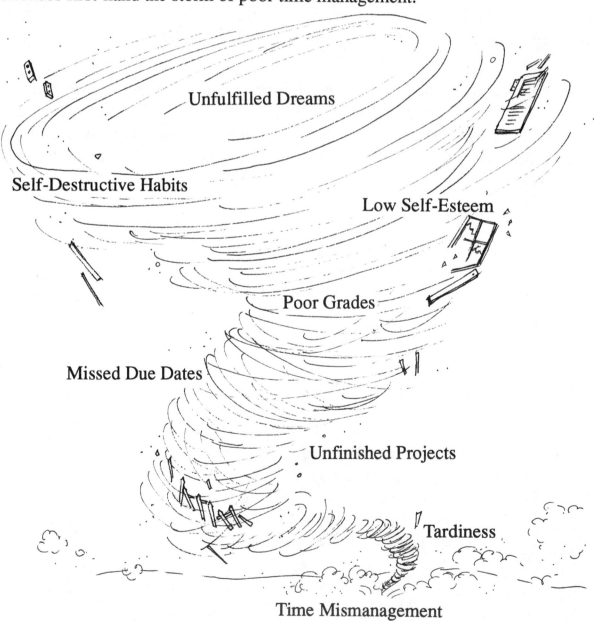

Unfulfilled Dreams

Self-Destructive Habits

Low Self-Esteem

Poor Grades

Missed Due Dates

Unfinished Projects

Tardiness

Time Mismanagement

Student Teachers

Listed below are six ways that time management can improve our lives. Turn the tables on your students and direct *them* to teach this lesson. One simple approach is to write the benefits on index cards and place them in a box labeled "Time Management." Students draw a card from the box and explain the benefit listed to the group, giving examples from their own experience.

Or you may wish to bring some creativity into the classroom. Direct students to choose one of the six benefits as the basis for an independent project. Students may draw cartoons, write jingles or songs, develop skits and pantomimes, or teach an object lesson to the class (Example: student displays an ad for a big-screen TV and explains the connection with Benefit #6).

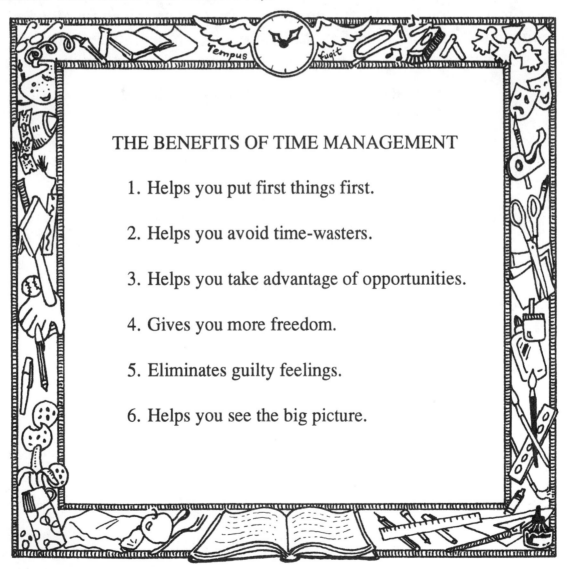

THE BENEFITS OF TIME MANAGEMENT

1. Helps you put first things first.

2. Helps you avoid time-wasters.

3. Helps you take advantage of opportunities.

4. Gives you more freedom.

5. Eliminates guilty feelings.

6. Helps you see the big picture.

The Great Equalizer

Over the years, people have seen a similarity between life and games of chance. So many of our personal circumstances are beyond our control; our genetic make-up is as random as a roll of the dice. There is, however, a great equalizer—time. We do not all have the same qualities and abilities, but we do have the same 24 hours each and every day. Often, the difference between success and failure can be measured by the amount of time we apply to a challenge.

Bring this truth home to students with a character analysis activity. Divide the class into small groups of three or four students and provide a die for each group. Students roll the die to determine the abilities for a character they create. The first roll determines how much intellect, the second roll determines talent, and the third roll indicates other advantages, such as family background or attending a good school. Tell students that the fourth roll—for time—has been predetermined for all groups. It is a 6, the maximum amount. Based on the numbers they rolled, students write assessments of their characters' potential and how they should best use their time.

Quality	Amount Rolled
Brains	3
Talent	1
Advantages	6
Time	6

Gorgeous George has a little musical talent and average intelligence, but he has the advantage of being very handsome. Because of his good looks, he is very popular. Students often elect him for class office. It would be easy for George to rely on his looks, but his friends would soon learn that he is not really smart enough for the job. If George puts his time to good use, however, he can study and learn as much as the "brains" in the class, to become a truly great leader.

After the groups have shared their fictitious characters, encourage students to do some private personal assessment. How do they rate themselves on the variables of brains, talent, and advantages? How can they use the great equalizer, time, to make the most of what they have? How can time help them overcome what they lack?

An Hour's Worth

From the perspective of youth, time appears to be an inexhaustible resource, stretching out in tedious hours of schoolwork and chores. Anyone over 20, however, knows that time is our most precious personal resource, not to be squandered. Use some math problems to help your students view time in a new light.

1. How many hours are there in one year? (8,760)

2. If you live to be 65 years old, how many hours will you have to live? (569,400)

3. How many hours does a 65-year-old person have to spend after graduating from high school? (411,720—assuming he or she graduates at 18)

4. For most people, one third of the time, 8 hours a day, is spent working. How many total hours will a 65-year-old person have worked? (137,240—assuming he or she begins working at 18)

What are students' responses to these numbers? Does a lifetime seem very long when expressed in hours? More importantly, do any of us have any time to waste?

Metaphorically Speaking

Compile a collection of illustrated metaphors to remind your students of the importance of planning. Provide some examples for starters and direct students in writing their own figurative sentences. Then have them illustrate their metaphors and place them in a class scrapbook. Keep it handy throughout the year as a refresher for individuals who show signs of slipping into the pattern of "middle school drift."

A good plan is a light at the end of the tunnel.

A good plan is a map through the maze of life.

A good plan is a flashlight in a dark and scary room.

A good plan is a blueprint for the mansion of my life.

A good plan is a ladder out of the pit of despair.

A good plan is a recipe for success.

Alphabet Soup

Before delving into the specific techniques of planning for homework, school projects, and extracurricular needs (covered in depth in Chapters 5 and 6 of this book), make certain your class understands the principle of outcome-based decision making. Discuss three different approaches that will help students examine a challenge from all angles. Unless we look at the whole picture, even the best plans may not get us where we want to go.

ABC Planning - This method reduces all the details of a decision to three basic categories:

Step A is knowing what you have.

Step B is knowing what you want.

Step C is using what you have (A) to get what you want (B).

5Ws and 1 H - Reporters use this formula to write a good news story, but it is also a handy way to make certain you cover all your bases.

Who?   **Where?**

What?   **Why?**

When?   **How?**

The 3 Ds - When you are trying to decide **if** and **how** to do something, see which of these categories best applies:

Do not do it. The action is not really necessary in light of your overall game plan.

Do it quickly. Tackle the job right now, get it over, and move on.

Do it one step at a time. This is for big tasks, impossible to do all at once. Plan how to make them easy, taking things little by little.

After examining these three methods, provide students with some practice in applying them to the types of decisions they make every day in their own lives. Ask each individual to choose a personal situation and work through one of the planning methods. Students record the thought process on paper and then share it with the class for feedback and evaluation. How well did students think through the issues? Are they ready to do more specific planning, or do they need to do some more "big-picture" thinking?

Hare-Brained Ideas

Locate a copy of Aesop's fable of the tortoise and the hare to read aloud to your class. Then discuss with students how this story applies to setting a pace in any skill area—sports, school, friendship, career. People are often overly ambitious when it comes to planning, only to burn out after a too-fast start. Or, as the moral of the story puts it, "Slow and steady wins the race."

Play a game to help students recognize a healthy pace. Pass out small pieces of paper and enlist students help in developing situation game cards. Students fold their paper in half, writing on the front a "tortoise" or "hare" situation. Inside their folders, they identify the card as T or H and assign a value, from minus five points to plus five points. All "tortoise" plans merit positive points, while "hare" situations earn negative ones. Screen the completed cards for appropriateness.

To play the game, students pair up and take a stack of cards. In turn, one student draws a card and reads the situation, deciding whether it is a healthy "tortoise" plan or a "hare-brained" idea. Students open the cards to check and record their scores. Play continues until all cards have been drawn. The player with the highest score at the end of the game wins. See examples of game cards below.

I plan to get ready for basketball tryouts by practicing four hours every afternoon after school. And on Saturdays and Sundays, I will practice double sessions, eight hours a day. (Hare, -5 points)

To be ready for basketball tryouts, I will practice one hour every day after school. On the weekends, I will try to get in an extra hour or two. (Tortoise, +3 points)

I am going to read 10 novels this weekend so I can earn extra credit and pull up my English grade. (Hare, - 2 points)

I plan to read at least one chapter every night in addition to my regular English homework. (Tortoise, +5 points)

Stump the Drudge

What is the difference between drudgery and meaningful work? Attitude! Even the most monotonous job can be endured with the right perspective.

Divide your class into teams for a game of "Stump the Drudge." Draw a simple frowning face on the chalkboard, with space on either side for the teams to record their responses. To play, read aloud one of the following boring situations. Allow 60 seconds for students to come up with ways to make the job more tolerable. As each team quietly brainstorms, the team recorder jots solutions on the board. Call time and check responses, ruling out any unsuitable answers. Record the number of suitable answers each team brainstorms on the board beneath the Drudge. After several rounds in which you provide situations and judge solutions, turn the job over to a small group of students. This is the part of the game students like most!

You have to rake the leaves in your backyard. It is as big as a football field.

You have to find 30 library books on your science topic.

You have to mow your grandmother's lawn.

You have to walk your dog every morning and every night.

You have to deliver papers to 60 customers on your paper route.

You have to put 200 words in alphabetical order.

You have to baby-sit your holy terror brothers for four hours.

You have to weed the family garden and flower beds.

You have to look up 25 vocabulary words and write a sentence for each one.

You have to memorize a long speech to give in front of the whole school.

Wake Up, Bartleby!

Locate *Bartleby the Scrivener*, a film version of the classic story by Herman Melville, to show your students. Bartleby is a clerk employed to help copy by hand all the documents needed in a lawyer's office during the mid-1800s. At first, the young man does his work well, but soon he begins to turn down assignments, answering, "I prefer not to," to every request. Puzzled by his employee's attitude, the lawyer investigates and learns that Bartleby has no family, no interests, no life outside the building, and in fact even spends every night sleeping at the office. Attempts to fire Bartleby are unsuccessful, for he "prefers not" to leave the job. Finally, in a desperate move to rid himself of this strange creature, the lawyer moves his office to a new location. Bartleby quietly refuses to move out when the new tenants arrive, so he is arrested and placed in jail, where he dies, friendless and alone.

Help students discover the meaning of this unusual tale. Bartleby is an extreme picture of what happens when a person refuses to participate, refuses to reach out to other people, refuses to take responsibility for decisions and actions in his/her own life. Nothing can hurt Bartleby, for he has nothing to lose.

Are there ways in which many students today are like Bartleby? How often do we see the same blank stares, the shrug of the shoulders, the quiet answer to any question, "I don't know...." Whose responsibility is it to choose to get organized, to take control and work hard, in school and out, to risk failure for the hope of success? There are too many young Bartlebys walking the halls of our schools today! Perhaps viewing and discussing this film will help some of them wake up!

Student Reproducibles—Chapter Two

Climbing the Beanstalk—Answers: 1. E, 2. E, 3. I, 4. E, 5. I, 6. E, 7. I, 8. E. Students will enjoy brainstorming about the motivations of other storybook characters—Cinderella, the Three Little Pigs, Wee Willie Winkie, King Midas, Robin Hood.

A Word to the....—Answers: A fool and his time are soon parted. Time is money. Time and tide wait for no man. Lost time is never found again. Time is the most valuable thing a man can spend. A stitch in time saves nine. Learn to take care of the minutes and the hours will take care of themselves. Challenge students to find other sayings and quotes about time management. Post them on your bulletin board.

Act/React—Answers: 1. A, 2. B, 3. B, 4. B, 5. A. Pair students up to develop some more active/reactive situations. Watch for current events articles that are good examples of the choices people make every day to act or react.

Heads or Tails—Actual student responses will vary. Example: 1. Active Response—Review throughout the week, just in case the teacher gives a quiz. Reactive Response—Panic when the teacher passes out the quiz, since you did not open your book once to review.

Taming the Beast—Answers: 1. N, 2. P, 3. P, 4. N, 5. P, 6. P, 7. N, 8. N, 9. P, 10. N. Roleplay other situations in which small positive rewards are effective—a baby-sitter and a stubborn child, a coach and his/her players, a physical therapist and a patient relearning to use muscles.

Where Are You on the Road of Life?—Suggested statements about the map follow. Students' actual responses will vary. When you do not have a plan, you end up going around and around in circles. Life in the fast lane is one way to get ahead, but you cannot stop to smell the roses. There are many unplanned pleasures and benefits along the road. There are many different roads in life we can choose to take. Some lead to knowledge and experience; some lead to dead ends. To extend the use of the map, assign students the task of writing travelogues about their adventures on the Road of Life.

Captain's Log—With the class, compare students' completed time sheets. How much of their time is controlled by other people? How much is theirs, to use as they see fit?

Climbing the Beanstalk

Types of Motivation

There are many reasons for taking an action. Often, we choose to do something because of what other people think. This kind of motivation, which comes from outside ourselves, is called *extrinsic*. Extrinsic reasons motivate us to work—until the outside force, whatever it is, stops or changes. Then our motivation disappears. The strongest motivation comes from deep within ourselves. *Intrinsic* reasoning includes the true desires of a person's heart, his or her best daydreams, and long-range goals.

Help Jack decide *why* he should climb the beanstalk growing outside his window. Code each reason below **E** for **Extrinsic** or **I** for **Intrinsic.**

WHY SHOULD JACK CLIMB THE BEANSTALK?

_____ 1. To impress the villagers, especially the miller's daughter.

_____ 2. To make his mother happy.

_____ 3. To satisfy his own curiosity about what is at the top.

_____ 4. Because his sister dared him to do it.

_____ 5. Because he considers it a personal challenge, and he wants to do it.

_____ 6. To get his picture in the paper.

_____ 7. To prove to himself his climbing ability. It does not matter if anyone else sees him do it.

_____ 8. Because all the men in his family have been good beanstalk climbers.

A Word to the . . .

Proverbs

Here are some wise sayings about time, but the words are all mixed up. Unscramble them to read the skywriting correctly.

time are fool parted A and soon his.

money Time is.

and man tide no wait Time for.

never Lost found is again time.

valuable man is can the thing spend Time a most.

time nine in A saves stitch.

minutes of of the will Learn hours take take to themselves care and care the.

Act/React

Taking Charge

In the game of football, which player usually gets more of the glory—a quarterback or a defensive lineman? Sports fans go wild when quarterbacks *act,* when they call the plays, when they set up the action that takes place down the field. Defensive players, on the other hand, *react.* They respond to the plays others have made.

In sports, in school, in life, we are faced with this same choice. Will we *act,* take charge, control events? Or will we *react,* waiting until things happen before we respond? Most time-management crises arise when we react to circumstances rather than planning and controlling them.

Check your understanding. In the situations below, which are the *active* responses?

1. How do you clean your room?
   A. Little by little, so it never gets too messy.
   B. Wait until it has been declared a hazardous waste dump.

2. You are driving down the highway when you spot a car ahead weaving back and forth across the center line. What do you do?
   A. Stay behind that car, and wait to see what happens.
   B. Pass as soon as it is safe, leaving the possibility of an accident far behind.

3. In a tennis match, when do you start to move?
   A. After your opponent hits the ball.
   B. Before the other player hits it.

4. You notice your clothes are getting a little tight. What do you do?
   A. Wait to diet until you cannot get anything buttoned anymore.
   B. Start cutting back on snacks today.

5. When do you buy holiday presents?
   A. As you spot them throughout the year.
   B. At the very last minute possible, one hour before the store closes.

Heads or Tails

Taking Charge

Flip a coin for each school situation below. If you land on Tails, give a *reactive*, defensive response. For Heads, explain an *active*, take-charge attitude.

1. Friday, your teacher gives the class a pop quiz. She often does this at the end of the week.	2. You notice you have about 20 sheets of notebook paper left.
3. You want to wear your green sweater to school tomorrow.	4. You hear about the possibility of a big party on the same day that you are planning to work on your science project.
5. Your friend drops by your house for a surprise visit while you are doing homework.	6. You are starting to have trouble with your grammar assignments.
7. The local weatherman predicts snow and school cancellations for tomorrow.	8. Your teacher is having a baby soon. The class has already collected money and asked you to buy a card.
9. You fail a math test.	10. You need a permission slip and $3.00 for the field trip next week.

Name_____

Taming the Beast

Rewards

Reporter: That animal act is simply amazing! What is your secret, Monzo?

Monzo: I train myself the same way I train my tigers. Some trainers use a negative approach. They whip and scream and punish their animals. I take a positive approach. I reward my cats every time they do something right. That way, they enjoy working in the ring.

Reporter: And you use this positive approach with yourself as well?

Monzo: But of course! I must keep my body in shape for performing. However, I do not like to work out. So I tell myself something positive every time I go to the gym.

Reporter: There you have it, folks! Amazing Monzo and his secret of success!

COULD MONZO'S SECRET WORK FOR YOU?

Read the statements below. Code each one *P* for Positive or *N* for Negative.

_____1. If I do not pass this test, I will get kicked off the team.

_____2. If I finish my homework early enough, I can call my friend.

_____3. If I get an A on my report card, I will go bowling.

_____4. I will have to repeat Spanish if I mess up this semester.

_____5. For each chapter I finish reading, I will take a five-minute music break.

_____6. If I work hard now, I will be prepared for high school.

_____7. If I do not finish my report, I will not get to go to the dance.

_____8. My parents will ground me if I get bad grades.

_____9. I will give myself a pat on the back every time I do a good job on my homework.

_____10. If I flunk this course, my whole future goes down the tubes.

Where are you on the Road Map of Life? What
true statements can you make about your own life
from studying the map below? Pick at least three
locations and write a paragraph about each.

WHERE
The Road

Stormy Weather

Loafers' Lake

challenge creek

Good Habits

Failure Forest

DAILY PLAN PATH

Time Management Skills

No-Plan Circle

Positive Attitude

INDECISION INTERSECTION

SKIMPERS' SHORT CUT

START YOUR LIFE HERE

DEAD END

ARE YOU?
Map of Life

Captain's Log

Time Sheet

Ship captains maintain logs of every voyage they make, recording those details that affect the trip, such as winds, weather, and ocean currents. These logs then become valuable tools in planning future voyages.

Chart your daily course below. Then you can keep a lookout for the sandbars of wasted time that wreck your voyage!

A.M.

6:00 _____

7:00 _____

8:00 _____

9:00 _____

10:00 _____

11:00 _____

12:00 _____

P.M.

1:00 _____

2:00 _____

3:00 _____

4:00 _____

5:00 _____

6:00 _____

7:00 _____

8:00 _____

9:00 _____

10:00 _____

How much time did you spend
  eating?
  bathing/dressing?
  traveling?
  doing schoolwork?
  doing chores?
  enjoying TV, music, video games?
  talking on the telephone?

Goals and Decisions

The Beast on Your Back

Prepare the way for a unit on decision-making by first examining the problem of indecision.

Explain to students that indecision is like a beast in a nightmare. In the darkness of this dream, you cannot see what the beast looks like, but you feel its heavy paws and hot breath on your neck. You struggle to get free, but the beast clings tight, a heavy load on your back. As you step painfully forward, the beast gnaws on your neck, arms, and shoulders, chewing endlessly, driving you insane. The only way to get rid of the beast of indecision is to shine a bright light in its face and ask some hard questions, such as these:

- What decision am I avoiding?
- Why am I afraid to decide?
- Which would be worse, to make the wrong decision or never to decide at all?
- How much time and energy does my indecision waste?

Now assign your students the task of describing their own personal beasts of indecision. What nightmare creature keeps them from setting goals and making decisions? What does this beast look like? Why? Some students may choose to give written descriptions, others may want to draw, sculpt, or assemble their monsters. Regardless of the medium used, students will hopefully realize the need to face their decisions head on.

The Forest or the Trees?

We have all heard the old saying about the person who focuses on details: "He cannot see the forest for the trees." Use this proverb as the basis for a classroom activity that shows the difference between goal and task orientation.

Divide the class into two groups. The first students are "the trees," who look at every situation from a task or detail orientation. The other group assumes the viewpoint of "the forest," a whole-picture attitude. Describe a situation and ask each side to give appropriate responses.

- A person working on a jigsaw puzzle. (Task orientation would focus on the individual puzzle pieces; goal orientation would see the big picture.)

- An assembly line worker in a manufacturing plant.

- A chef who runs out of one item needed for a big feast.

- An athlete training for the Olympics.

- A pet owner training a new puppy.

- A quilter.

- A private on the battlefield.

- A janitor in a science lab where vital research is being conducted.

- A student writing a term paper.

Once students see the difference in the two points of view, discuss the merits of each. When is it most beneficial to be goal-oriented? Is there ever a time when being task-oriented is more helpful? Go back through the list of situations together and decide which attitude is best for each one. In reality, the secret to achieving our goals is to adopt whichever point of view will see us through to accomplishment.

Goal Grammar

Many students have difficulty setting goals that are specific, depending instead on expansive dreams about the future.

"Someday I am going to be a rich and famous basketball player, with fancy clothes and a sport car. I will have lots of important friends and fly all over the country, going to parties and games, giving speeches, accepting awards. . ."

"I would like to be popular at school, with plenty of fun things to do and lots of friends. Members of the opposite sex will like me and want to go out with me. The teachers will respect me, too. . ."

"I will be a big rock star and hang out with all the coolest musicians on the scene. My walls will be covered with platinum albums. . ."

"I am going to be one of the country's leading lawyers, making a huge amount of money on every case I try. . ."

It is hard to tackle wishy-washy goals, so use a quick grammar lesson to bring your students closer to reality. No matter how broad or long-range a goal, it can be reduced to its essence by phrasing it as a two- or three-word sentence—"Earn an A." "Win the game." "Build muscles." "Play the guitar." Stated in this simple manner, the fuzzy "wherever-do-I-begin?" daydream becomes a concrete achievable goal.

After students practice on the grandiose goals listed above, challenge them to look at their own personal ambitions. Does phrasing a dream in its simplest form help with motivation?

Under the Umbrella

Faced with a multitude of options, many students have trouble choosing those immediate activities that will lead to the achievement of a long-term goal. Use an old umbrella to illustrate the decision-making process.

Select a common long-range student goal—making an "A" for the semester, graduating from college, winning the science fair, getting a lead role in the school play. Write that goal on a paper label and tape it to the open umbrella. On cut-out raindrops, write various short-term goals, some of which will lead to the desired outcome. Students select only the appropriate activities to suspend from the ribs of the umbrella.

Hang the completed goal umbrella from your classroom ceiling as a visual reminder of the need to test every choice we make. "Does this activity belong under the umbrella of my long-range goal?"

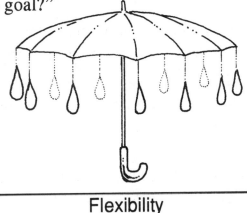

Flexibility

Not Set in Stone

Many students fear the consequences of setting goals. What happens if they do not make their goals? Are they doomed to fail forever? An "all-or-nothing" thinker wants to set goals permanently in stone, without regard for changing needs and circumstances.

Use the open-ended story starter below as the springboard for a discussion on goals, failure, flexibility, and taking chances. The best goal is one that makes room for the unexpected turns of life, while still bringing us to a desirable but perhaps different outcome.

Orgo, master builder, watched with pride as the final stone slowly slid into place. After years of back-breaking work, Stonehenge at last was finished.

The tribal chieftain walked up to the master builder. "Sorry, Orgo, the calendar plan is off. We've changed our minds. Your men will have to pull down all the rocks."

Orgo gulped. His golden dream of a beautiful stone calendar, to mark the passing of seasons for all time, crumbled to ash. But the builder was a quick thinker, and flexible, too. A new plan leaped to life in his brain.

"Just a minute, Zod. This stone circle is too beautiful to destroy. We could use it for. . . ."

Counting the Cost

Fair Trade

Shed a little poetic light on the subject of goals. Read "Barter" by American poet Sara Teasdale with your students. In this brief and well-known poem, the poet lists some of her favorite things: ocean waves, faces of children, music, fragrance. She then urges her readers to barter all they have for these lovely things.

Teasdale's poem reminds us that every goal comes at a price. So often we leap into a new situation without considering the cost. Are we willing to pay the price, to do what it takes? Is the goal worth the cost?

Use the headings below to make a "Trade Sheet" for students to weigh the costs of achieving their goals.

What I Want	What I Have to Trade	Is it worth it? Why or why not?
Big muscles	1. My free time. I'll have to spend it in the gym, working out.	
	2. Junk food. I'll have to eat healthier food.	
	3. Pain-free living. I'll be stiff and sore at first.	

Too Good to Be True

Here is an assignment your students will enjoy—daydreaming!

Ask them to imagine a realistic school day during which everything goes exactly right. How would it feel to complete the perfect school project or report, no floundering around, no last-minute panic? To be on time and well-prepared for every class and activity? Provide sheets of decorative stationery so students can list each step of their ideal days and describe their smooth successes. Encourage students to make these fantasy days their goals by posting the sheets where they can read them every day. A dream really can come true, especially if you work hard enough at it!

The Yeast Rule

One of the toughest areas of goal-setting is planning for time needs. Many students set a goal with a date and then give up in frustration when that date arrives and the goal has not been met. The problem is that most of the time we grossly underestimate the time required to complete a project. Here is a scientific way to illustrate this tendency.

For the demonstration you will need one teaspoon of sugar, a small glass of warm water, one package of dried yeast, and a large tray. Place the glass on the tray to protect your desk top. At the beginning of class, inform students that you are mixing up a glass of major school tasks and goals. Add the sugar and yeast to the warm water and stir well. Let the mixture sit for about 30 minutes. When students see foam creeping over the rim of the glass, discuss The Yeast Rule of Time Management.

This rule states that life's big assignments, projects, and chores are just like yeast. While you are not looking, they swell to twice their original size. The only way to deal with yeast is with some yeast of your own. Simply double the amount of time you think you need to spend on a project, and you will come closer to a realistic time goal.

(This demonstration actually shows the fermentation process. The sugar solution provides food and water for the yeast cells, causing them to multiply. The yeast in turn breaks down the sugar into alcohol and carbon dioxide bubbles, producing the mess that is now overflowing on your desk!)

Flying High

Use a page from the pilots' training manual to teach the concept of accountability. Post the flight procedures listed below and challenge your students to draw their own parallels between flying and setting long-range goals.

Flight Procedures

Every pilot files a flight plan before take-off.

The pilot maintains radio contact during the flight.

The pilot gets clearance from the tower before landing.

Goal-Setting Procedures

Before taking action to achieve a long-range goal, decide on a plan with short-range checkpoints that will lead step by step to the goal.

As you work to achieve your long-range goal, check your progress periodically. Just as the pilot checks in with an air traffic controller to stay on course, you can discuss your progress with someone whose judgment you trust—your parents, a teacher or counselor, a friend, your minister, priest, or rabbi.

Even when your long-range goal is in sight, make a final check to be certain you will land in the right spot. Is this goal really where you need to be right now? Have conditions and circumstances changed so that another goal might be better?

The Excuse Machine

Assemble an assortment of paper plates, cups, cardboard tubes, and small boxes to stimulate creative thinking. Divide students into small groups and assign them the task of inventing the Perfect Excuse Machine. Students may use any additional disposable or cast-off items for their creations. These models do not necessarily have to be operational, but they must provide at least ten good excuses why people give up on projects, assignments, and goals. When examining these reasons, help your students to resolve to finish, to persevere to the end of their goals.

1. The work was too hard.
2. I got bored.
3. I did not want to do it in the first place.
4. I ran out of time.
5. I ran out of supplies.
6. Something else caught my attention.
7. I never decided what I wanted to do.
8. I was too busy with other things.
9. I decided my work was not good enough.
10. I got tired.

Hand-Made Happiness

Show slides of historic patchwork quilts to point out a trait that many of these old coverlets share—planned imperfection. Sometimes a corner patch would be done in a different color or in an alternate design. In other quilts, a small square of different fabric would be stitched into the solid-color backing. Experts have several theories about this. Some say it reflects the quilters' belief that man is not perfect, that something made by human hands would always bear a flaw. Others feel it was a way to work a personal touch into a common quilt design. Whatever the reason, those quilts that feature this unique trait are considered quite valuable today.

How does the story of imperfect quilts relate to setting goals? Help your students see that perfectionism can prevent us from attempting things in life. We are so set on being perfect, we will not accept anything less. And yet, what are the odds that our work will be perfect? Like the quiltmakers of old, we should learn to value our efforts for their uniqueness. Making a conscious effort to accept small imperfections will help eliminate the fear of failure.

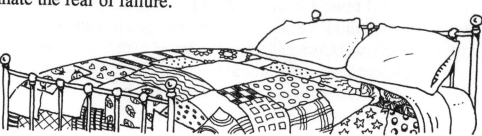

| Limiting Goals |

Victory Songs

Advertisers know the value of a song in conveying a message. Based on the success of ad campaigns, perhaps we should do more singing in the classroom! Challenge your students to come up with new lyrics for familiar tunes that express the important aspects of goal-setting. The musically inclined may wish to make tapes to share with the class. Or incorporate the songs into a student-written and produced video that you present to the school media center. The chorus might even consider including the songs in their next concert.

Did You Ever See a Student?
(Tune: "Did You Ever See a Lassie?")

Did you ever see a student, a student, a student,
Did you ever see a student with too much to do?
With lessons, cheerleading, homework, sports and reading,
Did you ever see a student with too much to do?

Oh, a Smart Kid
(Tune: "She'll Be Coming 'Round the Mountain")

Oh, a smart kid set himself just two big goals.
Oh, a smart kid set himself just two big goals.
He said, "This will keep me busy,
Anymore would make me dizzy."
Oh, a smart kid set himself just two big goals.

Oh, I Think I'm on the Road
(Tune: "If You're Happy and You Know It")

Oh, I think I'm on the road to great success!
Oh, I think I'm on the road to great success!
'Cause I have my goals in place
And I keep a steady pace.
Oh, I think I'm on the road to great success!

Oh, I see a little progress every day!
Oh, I see a little progress every day!
So I never start to worry
And I don't get in a hurry.
'Cause I see a little progress every day!

Previsualization

Mental Movies

To help students turn their goals into reality, teach them to make mental movies. The technique is actually known as previsualization, and it paves the way for success by putting the unconscious to work.

When faced with a challenging task, tell students to picture themselves successfully dealing with the situation. They are to imagine all the details from start to finish. They need to see themselves using behavior they would like to have in real life, succeeding in spite of some roadblocks. Once they have created their mental movies, they should play them back to themselves as often as they can. Using previsualization affects our thoughts and feelings, which in turn will help change our behavior.

For some fun with the concept of mental movies, duplicate the blank marquee and tickets on the previous page. Pass them out so students can create their own starring roles. Provide popcorn to munch on as you discuss the technique. Students will be interested to learn that people in all walks of life use previsualization—athletes, lawyers, actors, even doctors. The anesthesiologist who helped perform the first successful separation of Siamese twins, Dr. Mark Rogers, said he made mental movies of each step of the surgery for five months prior to the 22-hour operation. That's being prepared!

Keys, How to Use

Student Reproducibles—Chapter Three

Goal Pyramid—Paper project on planning steps to achieve goals, requires scissors and glue. For a follow-up activity, instruct students to bring pyramids back to class in one month so they can evaluate their progress with their goals.

Success Is . . .—Survey on definitions of adult success. After completion, assign students the task of developing a similar list of standards that define youthful success.

Passionate Pizza Project—Creative activity sheet; requires crayons or colored markers. As an art variation, ask students to create life-size models of their goal pizzas. Or use the home ec ovens and make edible versions!

Swiss Cheese, Please—Short-range goal setting; student responses will vary. Reinforce concept by distributing blank cheese diagrams with every major assignment. Help students form the habit of attacking large jobs in smaller pieces.

Pareto's 20/80 Principle—Prioritizing tasks by importance and results. Students' responses may vary; recommended are: Learning to Surf - #3, #8. Giving a Party - #1, #7. Doing a Science Project - #2, #10.

Happy Trails to You—Finding less-driven lifestyle; student responses will vary. Extend by challenging students to write additional "steamroller" situations.

Goal Pyramid

Tasks and Goals

The Egyptian pyramids have stood through centuries of wind and war to amaze us all. Archeologists still work to discover the exact building methods used. But one thing we know for certain: those ancient architects reached their goal of raising a breathtaking monument one building block at a time.

You can accomplish great things in your life the very same way. Cut out the pyramid below. Start at the peak and write in four long-range goals that you would like to achieve. Under each goal, write five tasks that will help you reach the peak. Fold on the dotted lines and glue the tabs together. Keep your goal pyramid on your desk at home so you will remember that big things happen one step at a time!

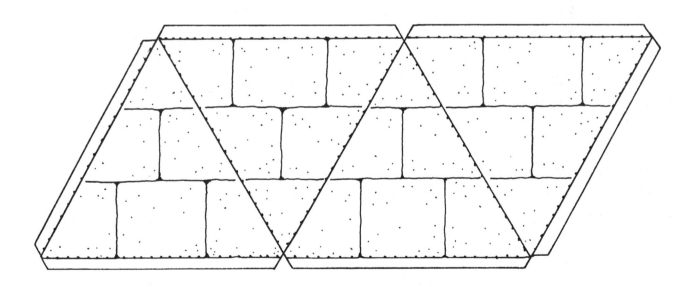

Success Is . . . .

Definitions

Everyone wants to succeed in life, right? But success means different things to different people. Use the checklist below to help you come up with your own definition of success.

Success in life is .....

_____ making lots of money.

_____ earning the respect of my family, friends, and neighbors.

_____ being debt-free.

_____ having authority and power over other people.

_____ providing a service or a product that someone else really needs.

_____ being my own boss.

_____ finding challenge and satisfaction most of the time.

_____ being well-known, famous.

_____ making enough money to provide for my family's needs.

_____ always learning and growing from my experiences.

_____ owning lots of nice things.

_____ being good at what I do, whether or not it makes me rich and famous.

_____ avoiding life's big problems.

_____ being happy every minute.

_____ making a difference in the world, no matter how small.

_____ having a family to love.

_____ being worry-free.

_____ developing a faith that helps me through life.

_____ having time for leisure activities.

_____ winning at everything I try.

_____ living a healthy lifestyle.

_____ having a few true friends.

_____ knowing everyone in town.

Next, think of your dreams and hopes for the future. Personalize your definition of success by completing this sentence:

In my adult life, I will know I am a success when _____

_____

_____

_____.

Passionate Pizza Project

Intellect + Emotion

Everyone knows that all pizzas begin the same way, with crust, tomato sauce, and cheese. But then passion takes over as the pizza maker adds toppings to the best pizza—mushrooms, pepperoni, sausage, peppers, onions, anchovies.

The same thing is true when an individual sets a personal goal. All goals start with the brainwork—the long-range plans, the steps to take, the short-range checkpoints along the way. But the best goals, the ones most often achieved, have lots of passion added to the basic recipe. Make yourself some Passionate Goal Pizza!

- Write your long-range goal on the crust.
- Write your plan of action in the center cheese area.
- Write your checkpoints in the outer tomato sauce.
- If your goal is a strong heartfelt desire, add pepperoni.
- If you spend time actively thinking about your goal, add mushrooms.
- If you dream about your goal, add sausage.
- If you read or talk to experts about your goal, add onions.

Swiss Cheese, Please!

Getting Started

Does the "bigness" of a project frighten you so much that you never even get started? Learn how to nibble your way to your goals!

First, break down your huge job into a series of smaller, more do-able tasks. Then whenever you have an extra moment, get one of these small tasks done and out of the way. Before you know it, you will have made big holes in your project!

Study the example at the right. Now think of a large project you face and fill in the cheese below with holes you can nibble away.

Pareto's 20/80 Principle
Smart Goals

Vilfredo Pareto was a scientist who lived in Italy in the 1800s. He was a wise man. He learned which of his goals were the most important ones. As he worked, he observed that 20 percent of his efforts produced 80 percent of his results. Pareto realized after much thought that the key to success was choosing the right 20 percent on which to concentrate. Make it your goal to use Pareto's Principle; work smarter, not harder!

See how the 20/80 rule applies to real life. In each list of activities below, find the two most important ones, those that will produce the most results.

Learning to Surf	**Giving a Party**	**Doing a Science Project**
1. Read surfing books.	1. Invite guests.	1. Do neat lettering.
2. Watch surf movies.	2. Plan food.	2. Experiment.
3. Get surfboard.	3. Design invitations.	3. Read about topic.
4. Get wetsuit.	4. Decorate room.	4. Make charts, graphs.
5. Take surfing lessons.	5. Plan games.	5. Decide on topic.
6. Watch other surfers.	6. Buy party favors.	6. Photograph results.
7. Buy surfboard wax.	7. Pick a date.	7. Make attractive display.
8. Get in water, practice.	8. Pick out clothes to wear.	8. Print report on computer.
9. Subscribe to surfing magazines.	9. Decide where guests sit.	9. Make report cover.
10. Study various surfboards.	10. Pick out music.	10. Write up results.

What large task are you facing? Write down every action you could possibly take in completing the task. Which 20 percent will yield the most results?

_____   _____

_____   _____

_____   _____

_____   _____

_____   _____

Happy Trails to You

Healthy Attitude

Working hard to achieve a goal is great, as long as you do not go overboard. There is a healthy difference between steamrolling to your destination and enjoying the journey. For each steamroller situation below, come up with a happier trail that will still lead to excellence.

Practicing in front of a mirror every morning, noon, and night, neglecting homework, skipping other activities to practice, telling friends that you will "just die" if you do not get the lead in the school play.

A happier trail: _____

_____

_____

Doing whatever it takes to make the Honor Roll, including cheating on tests, copying homework, pulling all-nighters, taking pills to stay awake and study, eliminating all leisure activities from your life.

A happier trail: _____

_____

_____

Becoming Mr. Popularity by joining every school club, running for many offices, being friends with people you secretly do not truly like, saying whatever people want to hear.

A happier trail: _____

_____

_____

Buying the right kind of mountain bike, even if it means using all your lunch money, selling your other nice things, stealing from your mother's purse, bullying your parents into buying something they really cannot afford.

A happier trail: _____

_____

_____

Rx for a Good School Day

Many schools encourage classroom visits from local professionals to build bridges with area business and industry. Enlist the help of a pharmacist or health care professional in presenting this important lesson on school preparedness.

Since the success of a student's school day is often determined by what happens at home beforehand, suggest that your guest lead a discussion on helpful ways to start the day. Provide empty gelatin capsules (available in boxes of 100 from a drug store) so the class can make its own daily "vitamin pills!" Students write suggestions on tiny strips of paper to roll up and insert in the capsules. Ask the school cafeteria to save you a large clear container so you can display this "Prescription for a Good School Day."

eriodically throughout the year, ask a student to open a capsule and read it out loud o remind the class of the connection between mornings at home and the school day.

Here is a starter list of tips to place in the capsules:

- Eat a good breakfast.

- Avoid foods with too much sugar. Sugar energy will run out around mid-morning.

- Get up early enough that you do not have to rush.

- Clear the deck mentally. Leave family problems at home.

- Take time to think through the day. Do you have everything you need?

- Get enough sleep to wake up feeling energized.

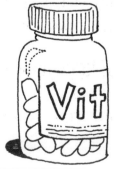

Courtesy Counts!

Part of feeling secure and comfortable with the school environment is knowing that boundaries exist to protect student and teacher alike. Whether you call it etiquette, good manners, or class rules, its basis is respect, for self and for others. Discuss with students the connection between courtesy, self-esteem, and time management. How does following accepted patterns of behavior actually save time?

Here are several ways to give your discussion of classroom boundaries a fun twist:

1. Write a list of desired behaviors on the board with the heading "It's a Zoo in Here." Assign students the task of rewriting the rules wild-style, such as "Please do not feed the animals." "Flap your wings before speaking!" "Attention all chimps, apes, and gorillas: No monkeyshines with chairs!"

2. Take a historical approach. Offer some examples of school etiquette that have gone out of style—wiping the dipper after taking a drink of water from the bucket, standing by your seat to answer in class, helping the teacher carry in wood for the stove. Next, send students home to find out about the classroom rules of their parents' and grandparents' youth. By comparison, modern rules seem very lenient!

3. What will school rules be like in the twenty-first century? Brainstorm with students on courtesy for the computer-linked classrooms of the future.

The Time-Saver Teacher

An old adage states, "More learning is caught than taught." Make certain you model time management principles in the way you conduct your classes.

Live your life out loud. As you set professional and personal goals for yourself, share your progress with students when appropriate; demonstrate the productive use of small minutes; treat your time with students as a precious non-renewable commodity; come to class on time and prepared.

You may want to develop your own Statement of Purpose, similar to the one below, to hand out to students and their families.

My Purpose as Your Teacher

I believe in the power of Knowledge to transform Life. I know this is true in my own life. Knowledge has given me skills, interests, friendships, hopes, and purpose where I had none before. This year I hope I can help you discover the Knowledge that will transform your life. To do that, I will come prepared to give you my very best every day, and I expect you to do the same. It is the most important work in the world that we do together, you and I.

| Knowing School Services |

Where, Oh Where. . .?

Part of helping the school day flow smoothly comes in knowing where to go to get help. Make certain your students are familiar with all the facilities and services available to them. Use the list below as a starter and add specific situations unique to your school. After students have identified these locations, challenge them to come up with additional school facility stumpers.

Where should you go here at school...

- if you forget your lunch?
- to sign up for extra tutoring?
- to borrow some red poster paint?
- if you want a good book to read?
- to find out the population of Manipur, India?
- to make a suggestion?
- to buy basketball game tickets?
- if your locker is jammed?
- to sign out to go to the dentist?
- to call home?
- if you have lost something?
- to have your temperature taken?
- to read a magazine article from the 1970s?
- to get your make-up work when you have been out sick?
- to find out about careers in music?
- if you need a Band-aid?

The Light at the End of the Tunnel

With today's emphasis on immediate gratification, endurance is a virtue that is frequently overlooked. Of all people, middle schoolers, notorious for their impatience and low frustration level, need to hear how others endure boredom and discomfort. Assemble a collection of inspiring biographies from your school library and offer a few facts about famous people to challenge your students. Here are some examples.

- Babe Ruth, homerun king with 714 hits, also struck out 1,330 times.
- Louisa May Alcott, author of much-loved *Little Women,* was told by her editor that she would never write anything that would be popular.
- Abraham Lincoln lost three elections, went bankrupt, and faced the death of his fiancée before being elected president.
- Walt Disney, who first worked as a newspaper cartoonist, was fired because his boss said he had no good ideas.

To enhance your discussion of endurance, cut a large dark tunnel shape from construction paper and place a small circle of light in the middle. Post on a bulletin board with the heading "The Light at the End of the Tunnel—What Kept You Going?" On index cards, students write sentences about times they endured pain, boredom, or difficulty to reach desired goals. Post the cards along with some guidelines, such as these:

1. Remember how good the outcome will be as you struggle.
2. Live one day at a time. You can endure anything for a short period.
3. Find something to enjoy in the midst of a difficult situation.
4. Tell yourself, "This will all be over soon. I will never have to do this again."
5. Remember the people who are counting on you to succeed.

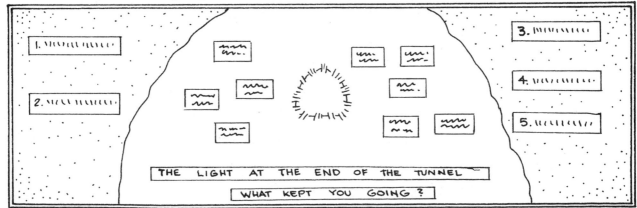

S. O. S. Coupons

In your classroom, S.O.S. stands for Stressed-Out Student, but help is on the way.

First, discuss with the class good ways to relieve stress during the school day, such as walking outside, breathing deeply, exercising during P.E. and lunch, getting to class early enough to relax for a minute.

Next, devise a system by which students can opt out of a limited number of regular class activities to take a Stress Break. Come up with alternatives for your Stress Corner that will provide some relief without distracting the class, such as listening to music with headphones, drawing, reading for pleasure, fixing a snack. Set up the guidelines students are to follow—one Stress Break per grading period, no Breaks during tests or key lessons, no leaving the room, one person at a time in the Stress Corner. Remind students that a Stress Break is only for their very worst days, when they really do not think they can cope. Often, just knowing an option exists is enough, but build some incentive into your program. Make and distribute S.O.S. coupons similar to the one shown below. Students may trade in unused coupons at the end of the grading period for bonus points or treats. The real reward, of course, is that they have learned to deal with their stress on their own.

Creative Covers

We often require our students to cover their textbooks for cleanliness' sake. But book jackets can also serve as effective school tools. Make them a beginning-of-the-year class project as part of your goal to help students build better study habits. Laminated paper, vinyl, or fabric all work well with any of the following additions:

- For storage pockets, make a deep fold in the cover material as you are wrapping the book. This forms a pocket on both front and back covers large enough to store papers. Another pocket possibility is the addition of a clear press-on pocket (available from an office supply house) or a library card pocket to hold smaller notes.

- Mount assignment book pages on the front on the book cover.

- If the cover is made of wipe-off material, consider using it as a place to write brief rules or reminders. Remove with a squirt of hair spray or duplicating fluid. (Make permanent markers available to students for in-class use only!)

- Use the cover to display incentives earned for class progress. Be creative in choosing incentives—cutouts from foreign magazines for a language class, or postage stamps from around the world (available in bulk at hobby shops).

Decide in advance on your book cover policy, including procedures for replacement. Provide materials as needed, or change covers halfway through the year. Tender loving care of textbooks begins with you!

Listening Skills
The Boy Who Listened With His Body

Read the story below to your class. As students listen, have them keep track of the different body parts (not counting ears) that are involved in classroom listening. How many ways does the protagonist use his body to facilitate listening?

The Boy Who Listened With His Body

Audi O. gulped as he read the sign on the classroom door, "Today's Special Presentation—World's Most Boring Lecture." His entire future, everything he dreamed of doing, depended on listening carefully for the next hour. It would be tough, but Audi knew just what to do.

First, he walked to a seat at the front of the room, near where the teacher would be speaking. Looking around, he nodded his head in satisfaction. "This is just the right spot," Audi said to himself. "Sitting here, I can hear easily, I can see the teacher in action, and yet I am far away from distractions like the door or a window."

While other students were chatting and throwing wads of paper at one another, Audi took a minute to focus on the lecture ahead. "I can play later," he thought. "But since my whole future depends on this class, I will use this time to clear my thoughts. H-m-m-m, exactly what do I need to learn from this lecture?"

The teacher entered the room, a huge stack of notes under his arm. He cleared his throat and jumped into a long and detailed explanation. Audi kept his eyes on the teacher. He wrote down key words and important facts in his notebook. Whenever he felt his mind wandering, he reminded himself to stay tuned in. Soon he could feel the knowledge pouring from his teacher's mouth right into his head. And it wasn't so boring after all!

Other students in the class were not so lucky. They stared out the window. They drew doodles and watched the clock. Fingers fidgeted and feet shuffled. When the bell finally rang at the end of the hour, most of them grabbed their notebooks and ran. Audi sat for a few seconds longer, writing.

"Hey, Audi! Want to shoot some hoops?" a friend called through the classroom door.

"Sure!" Audi replied. "Just give me a minute to finish my lecture notes. I write everything down while it is fresh. Later on, I think back about what the teacher said. I make sure I know why those facts are important."

"Oh, Audi, you're such a brain! Being smart just comes easy for you."

Audi shook his head at his friend. "I am not that smart, Gordon. I just know how to listen."

Students should come up with a list of body parts that facilitate listening similar to this one:

Eyes	To look at the speaker, to look over notes.
Brain	To clear before listening, to remind self to stay tuned in, to restate lecture afterwards.
Hands	To take notes, to stay calm.
Feet	To walk away from distractions, to stay still.
Posterior	To sit up close to lecturer.

Tricky Teasers

Jason Allsport's room was a mess. Dirty soccer socks hung from the foot of his bed. His closet door would not open because of the football pads piled on the floor. Rollerskates and a snorkel mask dangled from the door knob. Popcorn spilled out of a size 11 track shoe next to a bowling bag filled with soda bottles. "Y-e-s-s-s!" shouted Jason. "Another homerun!" He looked away from the television long enough to slamdunk a wad of paper into the miniature backboard taped to his bookcase.

Mrs. Allsport tapped on Jason's door. "Time out, son. What's all the racket about?"

Ask students to listen carefully for details as you read the paragraphs above out loud. Next, see if they can answer these tricky questions: Does Jason play tennis? (No.) How many sports does Jason like? (8) What are they? (Soccer, football, rollerskating, snorkeling, track, bowling, baseball, and basketball.)

Detailed passages like this one help students train themselves to be better listeners. Your class will enjoy developing tricky paragraphs and questions of their own to challenge one another. Detail-laden topics include foods, fruits, flowers, colors, number phrases, animals.

The Write Stuff

Many students make the mistake of buying assignment books that are too small and too flimsy. Typically, pages are hard to handle and tear out much too easily. Solve the problem by selecting as a faculty a notebook size and format that every teacher agrees to use throughout the year. Old-fashioned composition books are great because they are sturdy and have plenty of writing room. Or enlist the help of a local printer and design your own custom pad, complete with student art on the cover. Stock the assignment books in your school store; suggest that your parent-teacher organization sell them for a back-to-school fund raiser.

Next, plan a school-wide series of lessons on the assignment book, to provide practice in writing down homework and checking off tasks completed. Keep the formula simple—today's date, class name, and page number of work assigned, or an X if no assignment is given. One of the best ways to keep track of long-range assignments is to carry the due dates forward each day. Writing the assignment over again in the notebook keeps it foremost in our minds. Send a sample assignment entry home so parents will know what to look for in their children's notebooks. Check books weekly at the first of the year, to make certain everyone knows what to do. Later, make unannounced spot checks to keep students on their toes.

Taking Initiative

Camel Wisdom

Legend has it that when the world was new, the camel was given his choice of any spot on earth in which to live. Being an exceedingly wise beast, the camel chose the desert. Next, he was offered his pick from among all the foods the delicious young world had to offer. It was the camel's choice to eat salty desert plants and spiky thorns. When offered a life of ease, why did the camel make the hardest, least comfortable choices? To grow tough. And indeed, the camel did. Even to this day, with cars and jets crossing to every corner of the earth, there are still places so rough and dry that only the camel can get you there.

Use the example of the camel to encourage your students to take the initiative with their school day. Do they have a choice of countries in doing a social studies report? Choosing one about which little is readily available will sharpen their research skills; the resulting facts will be easier to write up, too, because there is not an abundance of information. Are they concerned about their progress in a particular subject? Teach them to ask for teacher feedback, to invite constructive criticism, to say, "How am I doing?" before or after class. Taking the initiative in this manner is a sign of maturity.

Making the harder choice when you do not have to is the wisdom of the camel.

Bookbag Maintenance

Let's Make a Deal

Students' bookbags are like black holes in outer space. Somehow, matter disappears into them, never to surface again!

Make cleaning out bookbags fun with this scavenger hunt game from the familiar television program, *Let's Make a Deal*. Surprise your students one day and ask them to place their bookbags on top of their desks. Next, distribute a list of the specific supplies and papers they should have in their bags. (Throw in some crazy items just for fun!) For every item on the list that students find in their bags, they receive one bonus point. For every out-of-date paper or piece of trash, they forfeit one point. The first time you do this, you will probably have plenty of laughter and lots of negative scores. The point to make to your students is that a sloppy bookbag filled with unnecessary items is an inefficient school tool.

This same game plan also works wonders with maintaining class notebooks!

Locker Management

The Bone-Chilling Knee-Knocker Locker

What better setting for a horror story than a middle-schooler's locker? First brainstorm with your class to list appropriate guidelines for locker usage. Then set students free to write wild tales in which every one of your locker laws is broken. This is lots of fun, and it gets the message across, too.

Locker Laws

1. Empty lockers of old papers and trash.

2. No food or pets allowed in lockers.

3. Stack books in locker according to class schedule.

4. To prevent theft, do not swap combinations.

5. Make certain locker is completely closed.

The Phantom of the Locker

It was a dark and stormy afternoon...

The Clean Sweep

Out with the old, in with the new! Begin each grading period with a "Clean Sweep Day," on which students take time to tidy notebooks, discard old papers, and file those they need to save throughout the year. Enlarge your sweep to include bookcases and files around the room, students' lockers and bookbags, your desktop.

As you work, you may wish to share this pearl of wisdom with your students: Don Aslett, multi-millionaire and owner of one of the largest cleaning services in the world, says, "I clean every chance I get—nothing restores order and dignity to human life like the act of caring for what we use."

Student Reproducibles—Chapter Four

The Best Teacher in the World—Open-ended sheet on student commitment to learning. Responses will vary. Collect and return to students periodically during year to revive flagging spirits.

The Attitude Well—Survey on personal traits. Student responses will vary. Extend by planning with class ways to improve poor attitudes.

Cultivating Kindred Spirits—Sheet to encourage relationships between students and faculty. Responses will vary; students may wish to keep their answers private. Encourage students to take the first step in cultivating their own "kindred spirits" at school.

Keys to Success In...—Class information sheet. May be used on a school-wide basis. Duplicate enough copies for students to have a sheet for each core subject and elective.

Banneker's Best—Using class time wisely. Answers: 1. S, 2. N, 3. W, 4. T, 5. C, 6. H, 7. D, 8. O, 9. G, 10. I, 11. A, 12. N. Code at bottom: WASHINGTON, D.C. To extend activity, assign task of rewriting time-wasters so they become time-stretchers.

Six-Weeks Calendar—Open calendar blocks for planning an entire grading period's work.

Alien Invader's Handbook—Classroom note-taking. Answers: A. 4, B. 11, C. 1, D. 7, E. 12, F. 9, G. 6. Students will enjoy writing guidelines for other study skills using similar approach.

Leonardo's Lists—Open daily list sheet, limiting goals per day to achievable number. Encourage extra research on da Vinci's inventions. Show a copy of his notebook pages in discussing private notes.

The Best Teacher in the World

Responsibility

Who is your best teacher? You are! That is true for every student, from kindergarten to college. Most people never realize this and waste time blaming others for the subjects they do not master. When you can take responsibility for your learning, you are on the road to true wisdom!

Read the statement below and then decide what commitments you will make to become your own best teacher.

I am the best teacher in the world, and my job is of vital importance—to take charge of my own education. As my own best teacher, I decide what I learn and when I learn it. I know that learning is more fun and more meaningful when I am in charge. I choose whether or not to cooperate with those in my life who want to help me learn. They can place knowledge before me, but they cannot force me to open my mind. I am in charge.

Because I am my own best teacher, I commit to doing these things every day:

_____

_____

_____

_____

_____

_____

_____

_____

_____

_____

_____

The Attitude Well

Positive Thinking

A good attitude is a person's greatest natural resource. It is as plentiful as water and as precious. A drop of good attitude brings life and growth and pleasure. Because anyone can possess a good attitude, we often take it for granted. We waste it on small, unimportant things; we let our wells become polluted with trash and negative thoughts.

How is the water in your attitude well? Put a check by each statement that applies to you.

_____ I look my teacher in the eye when he or she is speaking.

_____ When I have a choice, I sit toward the front of the classroom so I will not miss anything.

_____ I have a pleasant expression on my face.

_____ I have alert, not slouchy, posture.

_____ I come to class expecting interesting things to happen.

_____ I ask questions once in a while.

_____ I answer questions once in a while.

_____ When I do not understand something, I speak to the teacher after class.

_____ I take advantage of the extra review sessions my teacher offers after school.

_____ I volunteer when the teacher needs someone to participate.

_____ I believe that no learning is a waste of time, even when I do not enjoy the subject.

_____ I believe that the better my attitude is, the better my school day will be.

Now total your checks and see how you rate:

Less than 7	Call the Pollution Police! You need a new well!
7-9	See if some trash has blown into your well. Water shows slight impurities.
10-12	Congratulations! You have sparkling healthy water in your attitude well!

Cultivating Kindred Spirits

Seeking Help

Anne Shirley, the main character in *Anne of Green Gables,* was an orphan. Lonely without a family, Anne learned to find "kindred spirits," people to whom she could go when she needed advice or a shoulder to cry on. Anne's kindred spirits came in all shapes and sizes—old Matthew who never spoke much but listened carefully, Diana Barry who shared Anne's love of romance, and Mrs. Allan, the minister's wife.

We all need kindred spirits, especially at school. Have you worked at being friends with any of the adults who are here at school to help you? Try it! You might be surprised at the difference it makes.

In the blanks below, write the names of three adults at school whom you might consider "kindred spirits."

1. _____

2. _____

3. _____

If you needed help with a situation, which of these kindred spirits would you go see? Beside each statement, write 1, 2, 3, or *N* for none of the above.

_____ You are having trouble with your boyfriend or girlfriend.

_____ You just do not understand equivalent fractions.

_____ There is a group of kids teasing you and making your life miserable.

_____ You are very worried about something that is happening at home.

_____ You do not know which elective to choose for next year.

_____ You want to find out more about a hobby, interest, or career.

_____ You need a school recommendation for your scout awards committee.

_____ You want to change your entire class schedule.

_____ You have come up with a plan to help make your school better.

Name_____

 **Keys to Success In . . .**
Class Information

Keys to success in _____

Teacher_____Time _____

I am required every day to bring

_____

_____

_____

Tests will be given _____

Major assignments for the year are _____

_____

Rules for this class are

_____

_____

_____

If I miss a class, I must _____

_____

Extra times to see my teacher are _____

_____

My grades each marking period will be based on _____

_____

My study buddy is _____Phone _____

Banneker's Best

Using Class Time

In 1753, a young African American showed the world how to make time really matter. Benjamin Banneker, a self-taught genius in math, built the first clock made in America. Using gears carved from wood, Banneker's clock kept perfect time for over 40 years, and brought the 20-year-old inventor an opportunity to correspond with Thomas Jefferson.

Listed below are typical classroom behaviors. Decide if each is a time-stretcher or a time-waster and circle the appropriate letter. Then use the code letters to find the name of the city Banneker planned and surveyed.

Classroom Behaviors	Time-Stretchers	Time-Wasters
1. Cleaning out your bookbag in study hall.	B	S
2. Copying down tomorrow's assignment from the board as soon as you get to class.	N	U
3. Using time before class to review homework.	W	J
4. Drawing terrific doodles.	E	T
5. Listening carefully during class.	C	K
6. Skipping over the test directions.	P	H
7. Using a free period for a social hour.	A	D
8. Reviewing before a test during lunch.	O	F
9. Taking a nap after you turn in your paper.	Y	G
10. Taking good notes in class.	I	M
11. Livening up a dull class with silly comments.	V	A
12. Daydreaming about your fabulous future.	R	N

__ __ __ __ __ __ __ __ __ __ __ __
3   11   1   6   10   12   9   4   8   2   7   5

Six-Weeks Calendar

Scheduling

Use this calendar for planning your schedule for the entire grading period. Write correct dates in the corner blocks.

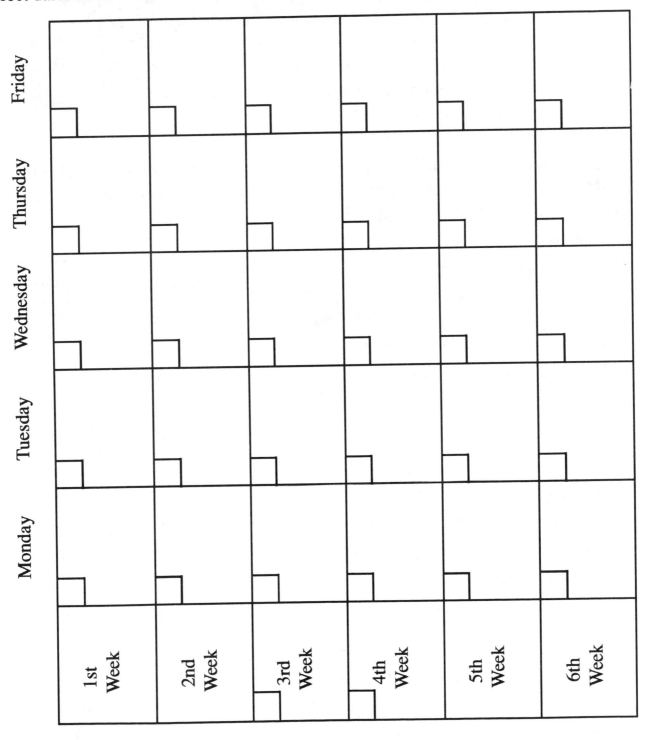

Alien Invader's Handbook

Note-taking

My dear Wrozko,

After you land on Planet Earth and secure the proper articles of clothing, head for the Earthlings' house of learning. (They call it a *school*.) You will observe the young humans engaged in an activity called note-taking. Study the rules below carefully, and soon you will pass as an Earthling student. May the winds of Jupiter be with you.

Your Interplanetary Advisor,
Sasmillian

1. Earthlings take classroom notes to organize the vast assortment of facts their teachers throw at them each day.

2. Earthlings' class notes are different from notes they take for a report. They are usually less structured, not as detailed.

3. So you will not reveal your identity as a non-Earthling, practice your note-taking skills before you go to their school. Write down the main ideas as you listen to their television news. Take notes when you listen in on an Earthling family discussion or meeting. Play listening games with the other trainees from Jupiter.

4. Always, I repeat, always go to Earthling school prepared to take notes. You will need something called a *looseleaf notebook*, lined paper, and a writing device known as a *pencil*.

5. At school, listen for note-taking clues, such as "The three reasons are . . ." "Five ways that . . ." "The point is. . . ."

6. Leave lots of white space on the page as you take notes. This is not for doodles of your home planet, but to make additions or corrections later.

7. You will not have time to write down word for word everything the Earthling teacher says. Just put ideas in your own words.

8. Do not worry about Earthling spelling. You can (and should, dear Wrozko!) correct that later.

9. Use abbreviations, symbols, and diagrams to capture the main ideas. Make certain, however, you can remember the meaning of any abbreviations you use. And please, do NOT use the Jupiteranian alphabet. This could give away your identity as a secret alien invader.

Name_____

10. Write down any examples that the Earthling teacher gives. These will be useful when you study for your Interplanetary exams.

11. Define any special terms or procedures that the teacher uses. How else will you learn to think like an Earthling?

12. After class, review your notes. Underline the most important ideas. Reorganize and rewrite anything that did not get written down correctly. See if you have questions for the next day of Earthling school.

The tattered document above was found beside a cassette tape labeled "Interviews With Earthling Students: Wrozko Niibur 77854." Which of the note-taking rules are the human students discussing? Write the rule numbers on the lines.

_____A. "I hate to waste paper, so I write my class notes on the backs of old worksheets or whatever I happen to have handy."

_____B. "Today I took notes on the distributive property of addition over multiplication. But I did not write down what it means, so. . . ."

_____C. "Notes? Who bothers to take notes? I can keep everything sorted out in my head. The commutative property is a form of government, right?"

_____D. "I write down exactly what the teacher says. I may not understand it, but I write down every single word."

_____E. "Look over my notes this afternoon? Why bother?"

_____F. "Hey, what do you think these abbreviations mean? I have no idea what I meant when I wrote "Npln ft btl Wlu.""

_____G. "I do my best artwork in my class notebook. Makes the white space look more interesting, you know."

© Frank Schaffer Publications, Inc.   73   FS-10168 The Organized Student: Teaching Time Management

Leonardo's Lists

Making Lists

Painting, anatomy, military science, math, physics, botany, astronomy, aerodynamics, civil engineering . . . no subject was off limits to Leonardo da Vinci. This Renaissance thinker developed hundreds of ideas for machines so far ahead of his time that scientists still work on his concepts today. How did he keep up with all his ideas? He did it in lists and notebooks, 4,200 pages of which still survive. Leonardo even wrote his private lists backwards so others could not read them easily.

Take a tip from Leonardo and make out your lists for the day's great accomplishments. (Writing forwards is acceptable!)

To Do Before School

_____
_____
_____
_____
_____
_____

To Do During School Day

_____
_____
_____
_____
_____

To Do After School

_____
_____
_____
_____
_____
_____

Structured Study Skills

Know Your ABCs

So often we rely on paper and pencil when there is an endless number of other ways to learn. Use this idea first to show your students the range of study possibilities, and secondly, to help them begin to see their own personal preferences.

Announce that the task for the day is to write "The ABCs of Learning About Anything." Students are to write the letters of the alphabet down the left side of a sheet of paper, skipping several lines between each letter. Then go back and provide examples of learning methods beside a letter or two. The goal of the students is to come up with at least 26 different activities, one or more for each letter of the alphabet. Compare the results so students can see that the number of ways to learn is practically limitless. Which methods are their favorites? Which ones have they never before thought to try?

Your class may want to compile an ABC book for the school library that will serve as a springboard for creative assignments. The interesting question is, will the teachers fight the students for it?

The ABCs of Learning About Anything

A   Act out scenes about your subject.
    Absorb excitement from others who like the subject.

B   Build a model.
    Believe you can master your subject!

C   Circle key words in your notes.
    Conduct a panel discussion on your subject.
    Create and cook a recipe related to your subject.

D   Draw a diagram.
    Design an invention related to your subject.
    Debate a topic with someone who holds a differing opinion on your subject.

E   Edit a newspaper on your subject.
    Explain your subject to a younger student.

F   Find everyday objects that symbolize your subject.
    Furnish a model on your subject.

G   Give a speech on your subject.
    Grade someone else's paper.
    Graph your results.

H Help someone else study.
Hang a poster about your subject where you will see it while you are in bed.
Haunt the library.

I Interview experts on your subject.
Imagine that you are an important person connected to your subject.

J Join a club on your subject.
Jump in with both feet!

K Keep an idea journal on your subject.

L Listen to tapes.
Learn the special vocabulary of your subject.
Launch a publicity campaign about some aspect of your subject.

M Move to music related to your topic.
Memorize poetry on your subject.
Mime your subject.
Mark important facts in your notes with bright colors.

N Name all the categories you can think of that are part of your subject.
Narrate a skit on your topic.

O Outline your subject.
Observe experts in the field at work.

P Photograph scenes related to your subject.
Pack a suitcase for some destination related to your subject.
Perform a comedy routine about your topic.

Q Quiz yourself on what you know about your subject.
Quilt a design related to your subject.

R Record a song on your topic.
Review a book.
Race with a friend to master a subject.
Raise as many unusual questions as you can think of related to your subject.

S Send letters requesting information.
Supervise a community project related to your subject.
Stuff a soft sculpture on your topic.

T Take a survey.
Throw a party using your subject as the theme.
Toast one of the heroes of your topic.
Taste a food related to your subject.

U   Underline important facts in your notes.
    Unravel a puzzle.
    Use a tool or technique related to your topic.

V   Visit a museum or display on your subject.
    Vote for your favorite part of the subject.

W   Watch videos and films on your subject.
    Wear a costume related to your subject.
    Wrap a present that would be suitable for
      someone connected with your topic.
    Write a will about the subject.

X   X-ray your subject. Look at it inside and
      outside, top to bottom, and from every possible angle.

Z   Zero in on details that fascinate you.
    Zoom to the head of the class!

| Brainstorming |

Build a Better Birthday Cake

Where do good ideas come from? Can a little creative thinking transform a commonplace assignment into an exciting one? Answer these questions with a demonstration of the technique of brainstorming. First, make certain you have plenty of chalkboard space, chalk, and a speedy recorder. Tell the class its job is to think of different and unusual ways to make a birthday cake. The cake does not have to be edible, but it must have a typical cake shape. All suggestions go up on the board, and at this stage no one is allowed to rule out any idea. Aim to get at least one response from every student in the class. Here are a few ideas.

- a cake carved from rock
- a cake made of firecrackers
- a cake covered with seashells
- a cake covered with fur
- a sand cake
- a cake covered with marbles
- a foam rubber cake
- a cake covered with jewels
- a round storage box painted to look like a cake
- a mirrored cake
- a cake covered with postage stamps
- a cake made of dog biscuits
- a cake covered with maps
- a footstool cake

When you have a board full of suggestions, go back and examine the possibilities. What uses or needs can students associate with the various suggestions? Would a dog like a cake covered with dog biscuits? Could a pet food company use this idea in its advertising? Who would use a fake cake made from foam rubber? A baby? A magician? A clown? Would a bakery buy this to put in its front window instead of wasting a real cake? The technique of brainstorming works well with more traditional assignments, too. Discuss how students could brainstorm topics for a composition, a science project, or a social studies report.

Types of Learning
Light Bulbs and Beehives

To show the flash of a good idea, many cartoonists draw a light bulb beaming over a character's head. The image is appropriate. Often, learning does come in quick, intense, "A-ha! I've got it!" moments. Light bulb learning is very exciting. We find ourselves comprehending material in big chunks and moving forward rapidly.

But our understanding of the learning process would be more accurate if we added a second image, that of the beehive. Beehive learning comes little by little, gathered from a variety of sources. In this type of learning, there is no single moment of discovery, light bulb style. Instead, there is a string of smaller discoveries, each one leading to the next. Many times our frustration in learning comes because we are looking for the light bulb moment instead of trusting in our beehive routines. It is a fact that, in school and in real-life situations, most skills are developed one small step at a time.

Challenge your students to review on paper a significant learning experience of their own. Was it light bulb or beehive learning? How did it feel? What happened as a result of the experience? Understanding both kinds of learning will help anxious students relax.

Carpe Minutum

Thanks to the movie *Dead Poets' Society,* many students are familiar with the Latin maxim, *carpe diem*. Expand Horace's thought with some Latin of your own, *carpe diem, carpe horum, carpe minutum* ("Seize the day, seize the hour, seize the minute.")

Many students wait to begin their studying until they have big blocks of uninterrupted time. Meanwhile, minutes of valuable time slip away. Challenge your students to examine their own use of life's little minutes. How many science terms could they learn waiting at the orthodontist's office? Could they think of a topic for their English composition during a long bus ride home? Do they jump into homework when they have a bonus free period?

Some people fit life around studying; others fit studying around life.

And the Winner Is . . .

Here's a way to take a light-hearted look at a nagging problem—wasting homework time. First, give a few examples of classic student time wasting—daydreaming, snacking, talking on the phone. Then ask how many in the class consider themselves champion time-wasters. In turn, the candidates describe their best ways to kill time. Stories may be a bit exaggerated, but that will help get your point across. After all accounts have been given, ask the class to vote by applause for the person to hold the title "Best Teen Time-Waster of 199_." Follow up with a discussion of ways your winner can conquer his or her study time-wasters.

Below is a starter list of typical after-school activities. Some are necessary and unavoidable; others are healthy forms of recreation but can fall into the time-waster category when carried to excess.

baby-sitting	doodling
walking home	doing chores
snacking	practicing music lessons
playing sports	talking with parents
watching TV	attending meetings, team practices
riding bikes	talking on phone

showering   trying on clothes
caring for pets   being with friends
playing video games   reading newspaper, magazines
shopping   resting
reading novels   daydreaming

Join the Club

Just for fun, provide students with the address of The Procrastinators' Club of America. A legitimate organization, it was founded in 1956 "to promote the fine art of procrastination." The club holds meetings, but only on an irregular basis, and usually behind schedule. Your class may wish to subscribe to the club newsletter which arrives about a month late. Write to:

The Procrastinators' Club of America, Inc.
1111 Broad-Locust Building
Philadelphia, PA 19102

Roll-a-Room

Out on the job, a young worker quickly learns that his/her success depends on tools and supplies—having the right tool at the right time, with the right materials needed to complete the task. The job of studying is no different. The right study environment can mean better concentration, more enjoyment of learning, and better grades. Use this exercise to stimulate students' thinking about their own best places to learn.

Distribute copies of the grid on the next page, along with a six-sided game die. Students roll to select a feature in each category. Then they are to write a personal evaluation of those particular features. Are they the best ways to enhance learning for them? Would other features be more beneficial? Designing a space that is conducive to our own learning style strengthens our commitment to learn.

	1	2	3	4	5	6
Sight & Sound	absolute quiet	elevator music	rock 'n' roll	no visual distractions	a window to look from occasionally	interesting surroundings
Social Level	study alone	study over the phone	study with a friend	study with a parent	study surrounded by family	study with a combination of social levels
Supplies	pencils and pens	colored markers	ruler	lined paper	drawing paper	eraser
Resources	dictionary	textbooks	a neat notebook	assignment book	teacher handouts	bookbag
Extras	book case	box or drawer for storage	computer	encyclopedia	other reference books	calculator
Furniture	a desk or table	firm, comfortable chair	good light	bed to study on	pillows for propping	bulletin board

Study Interruptions

Do-Not-Disturb Signs

Sometimes a little thing can make the biggest difference. Provide the materials for your students to make signs to hang on the door of the room at home where they study. Regardless of the slogans or artwork, the signs are a way of announcing, "I take my homework seriously. Please respect my efforts."

Enlarge the pattern below and provide some starter ideas, along with markers and posterboard. Tie in your curriculum by requiring students to write subject-related slogans. Laminate the completed signs if possible.

"I can't leave for Kitty Hawk yet, Orville. I'm still working on my HOMEWORK!"

"I have nothing to offer but blood, toil, tears, sweat, and HOMEWORK!"

"Fourscore and seven years ago, I started my HOMEWORK."

"It was the best of times, it was the worst of times, it was HOMEWORK time!"

"Listen, my children, and you shall hear,
The sound of HOMEWORK, loud and clear!"

"I think, therefore I DO HOMEWORK!"

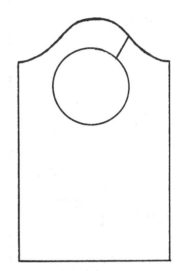

TV/Telephone

The Terrible Twos

Of all the after-school time wasters, two seem to swallow hours of study time—the telephone and the television. Assign students the task of keeping a log for one week of the time they spend on the phone and watching TV. The results will astound you all!

After your class has looked at their log figures, give them this creative challenge—to come up with a way to portray these two American pastimes as terrible time-gobbling monsters. Artistic students may wish to draw cartoons of the Terrible Two in action; some will want to write poems, interviews, or stories; others may work in small groups to develop skits, pantomimes, even rap performances.

Anyone can conquer the Terrible Two with some decision making beforehand. Students should decide exactly *when* they will take phone calls or watch TV. They can also set a *limit* on the length of time they spend. By giving some thought to the problem ahead of time, even TV and telephone zombies can break the control these monsters have over their lives!

Kitchen Timer Management

Here is a little study tip to share with your class. Suggest the use of a wind-up kitchen timer to pace studying at home. Students who tend to rush through assignments and make careless errors should set a time slightly longer than they think they will need. Then they discipline themselves to stick with the assignment until the timer goes off. Students with the opposite problem, dawdling, should set a reasonable time and then try to beat the clock.

Posture

Body-Mind Games

When your class needs a brief change of pace, take a few minutes to demonstrate the effect posture can have on a person's learning. Ask two actor volunteers, one male and one female (who do not mind looking a bit silly), to come to the front of the room. Each is to assume a posture as you describe it.

Instruct the first student to sit at a desk with back straight and shoulders squared, arms resting comfortably on the desk, feet flat on the floor. The picture at this point should be of a serious-minded student ready to study. Now comes the hard part. Tell the student to let the eyelids droop, drop the chin, and rest the tongue on the lower lip. Your volunteer will discover that this facial expression is hard to achieve when the body has assumed this pose.

The second actor will work for an opposite effect. Instruct him to sprawl in a chair, leg across one knee, elbow propped on a neighboring chair, head resting on hand. When his body expresses complete relaxation, ask him to look very alert, with wrinkled forehead and narrowed eyes. Why is this so hard to do?

Discuss with students the connection between mind and body. Our bodies send to our brains strong signals which have a real effect on our mental activity. Anyone who has ever been sick knows this is true. But our bodies also influence our brains in a positive manner. If you are not in the mood to study, try getting into a studious posture first. Your body will fool your brain into thinking it is ready to work.

Handling Mental Blocks

Detour Ahead

Give the challenge below to a small group of students who work together to prepare a sound-effects skit. Schedule the performance during a week when the class is busy with big research projects. The best learning takes place when students teach themselves!

It happens to everyone—you are hard at work writing a big report when you suddenly run into a mental roadblock. No ideas will come, your brain is blank, nothing makes sense. Do you hit the panic button and fall apart? Do you quit in disgust? No. You simply take a detour. Shift to another job related to the task, like designing the report cover or writing the bibliography. Give your brain something different to think about for a few minutes. Then when you go back to writing, the roadblock will be down.

Your mission is to create a pantomime that will communicate the concept above through sound effects. You may use a narrator if you wish, but no other speaking parts. Please control the loudness of the sounds you use; we do not want to disturb other classrooms. Thanks for tackling this challenge!

Stress Breaks

The Study Machine

Meet Rita May Green, the study machine,
The studying-est girl you've ever seen!
She studies through breakfast,
She studies through lunch.
She doesn't miss food—

She's got pencils to munch!
And numbers to juggle,
And papers to write.
Rita works long into the night.
She won't take a break,
She might make a mistake,
So Rita keeps working, hour after hour,
A study machine turned up to full power.
Rita May Green thinks she's doing all right:
She aims to be a great study-er.
But without any breaks, the facts in her head
Just get muddier...
     and muddier...
       and muddier...

Use this poem to inspire other creative works that illustrate the importance of study breaks. You might end with an entire book of silly verse and wacky drawings on balancing homework with relaxation.

Reading to Learn

The No-Fail Formula

A common formula used to teach reading-for-meaning is SQ3R—Survey, Question. Read, Recite, Review. Play a familiar party game to have some fun with this study method.

First, write the formula on the board and give a brief explanation. Then go around the room and whisper one of the key words to each student. At a signal, the students leave their seats to make complete formula groupings. As they circulate, they may ask one question only, "Are you_____?" A yes/no answer is permitted. The game continues until all groups have been formed. (For groups that work out equally, play with multiples of five. Or give some students two key words so a complete formula can still be made with less than five students.)

Next, hand out copies of a sample textbook passage so the groups can practice applying the SQ3R formula. Each student explains his/her role in tackling the passage.

Cursive Cure

One of the sad facts of life is that teachers often judge written work in part by the quality of the handwriting. It is another fact that polishing penmanship is low on the list of middle school priorities. But it is never too late; with attention and practice, middle schoolers can improve their handwriting.

Choose an assignment once a month to give special emphasis to cursive writing. Provide various colored pens and unusual paper for students to use in completing their work. Pair students to critique each other's penmanship.

Even in this computer age, the handwritten word is still the most personal and intimate of communications. Will we ever put word-processed love letters under our pillows?

Lesson Plans

Human beings are masters of sensory learning. Since before birth, we have touched, tasted, smelled, listened, moved, and watched to discover information about the world around us. We never lose the capacity to learn through our senses, although our educational process does not necessarily cultivate them. Memorization is one skill that can be greatly enhanced by multi-sensory involvement.

Turn the tables on your students and let them plan a lesson for a change. First, select a task involving memory, such as learning spelling words, vocabulary definitions, scientific formulas, lists of names and dates. How many different *sensory* ways can students devise to master the memory work? Provide lesson planning sheets on which students write the various approaches. Discuss them as a group so everyone can benefit from new ideas about learning.

Task: Learning a list of spelling words

By writing— Copy the list by hand several times.

By speaking— Spell the words out loud. Put the words to music and sing them.

By touching— Make pipe cleaner letters of the words. Type the words on a keyboard. Shape the letters out of clay.

By listening— Tape yourself spelling the words. Listen frequently.

By looking— Make flashcards of the words. Review them often.

By moving— Spell out the words with your body, cheerleader-style. Put the letters to an exercise routine. Say the letters as you go through the routine.

Other— Make letters out of pancake batter and eat them!

Math Skills

A Handle on Word Problems

Word problems are often stumbling blocks, even for good math students. The words always seem to get in the way of the numbers! Here is a mnemonic device to share with your class. Have drawing paper and scissors available so students can make cutouts of their hands. Instruct them to label the thumb and fingers as shown.

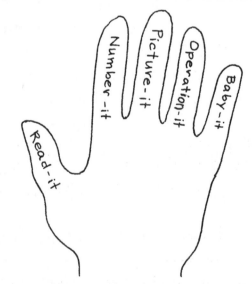

The thumb, Read-It, stands for the first step in attacking a word problem—to read it carefully. The pointer finger, Number-It, is to pick out all the numbers in the problem, including those written in words. The middle finger, Picture-It, stands for visualization—to picture the problem in your head. The ring finger is labeled Operation-It—to look for the operational words in the problem and to decide what they mean. Phrases such as "total," "in all," or "altogether" indicate addition or multiplication. "How much is left" or "how much older than" call for subtraction, and "how much each" for division. The last finger, Baby-It, is an extra step to take if you still do not understand the problem. Substitute smaller numbers for the large ones and see if it makes the problem clear.

Once students take these five steps, they should have a handle on how to solve any word problem. Encourage students to keep the cutouts in their math books so they can refer to them often. Soon the procedure will seem like second nature.

Revising

Mary Poppins Slaps Willie Nelson

One of the most important steps in completing a big project is one that is most often omitted—revision. Revisions are difficult to make for several reasons, including lack of time, impatience, frustration in spotting errors. There are, however, some methods students can use to make the job of revision less painful.

First, teach students to always read their rough drafts out loud to themselves. Errors in sentence structure surface best this way. Second, if students have access to a word processor, suggest that they do their writing on it. The ease with which changes can be made certainly beats recopying a long composition by hand several times. Third, teach perfectionist students to borrow a term from computer programming, *de-bugging*. Some students get so discouraged in the revision stage, they throw out the entire paper instead of looking for the small troublesome spots. Revision is all about saving what is good and de-bugging what is not.

To help students focus on the different aspects of proofreading, give them this humorous acrostic—Mary Poppins Slaps Willie Nelson. The first letter in each word of the acrostic stands for a necessary area of revision.

M - Meaning: Does the writing express what I want it to say? Are the facts correct?

P - Paragraphs: Did I indent? Are my paragraphs made up of related sentences that focus on a single idea?

S - Sentences: Did I use complete sentences, with capital letters and correct punctuation?

W - Words: Are the words spelled correctly? Did I choose the best words for my meaning?

N - Neatness: Have I followed format directions? Is it easy to read?

The acrostic is a handy way to remember the checklist above, but you do not have to stick with this particular one. Students may enjoy creating their own personal memory devices for the procedure. Maybe, Muddy Penguins Slurp Wet Noodles!

Organization Information
Structural Models

Outlining and clustering, also known as idea-webbing, are the two methods we teach for organizing information. Make three-dimensional models of these formats to help students better understand each. For the outline model, pick a simple example from your textbook and reproduce the pattern by stringing various sizes of large beads. For the model of a cluster, build a corresponding web of toothpicks and small gumdrops.

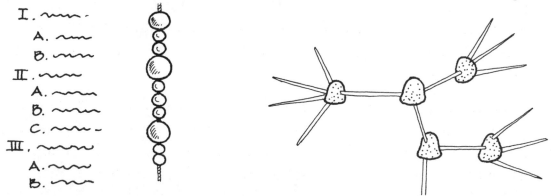

Discuss with students the need to match topics with the most suitable organizational format. Those subjects that are well-defined, linear, with some type of order or sequence, are most easily outlined. Topics that lend themselves to clustering are more open-ended and flexible. Information may be complex, with branches in many different directions. Give students the following list of situations and lead them to determine which organizational format would be best for each.

- A news reporter taking notes at a puzzling crime scene. (cluster)
- A news reporter taking notes at a pre-planned school board meeting. (outline)
- A student writing on the three categories of rocks. (outline)
- A student writing on the current music scene. (cluster)
- A baker writing down everything he knows about making a cake. (outline)
- A traveler writing down everything he knows about a country he has visited. (cluster)
- A scientist trying to come up with a new use for a substance. (cluster)
- A scientist reviewing everything that led to the discovery of a substance. (outline)

Point out that often a cluster is the first step in organizing facts, followed later by a more defined outline. Encourage students to add personal touches to their organizational formats—symbols, small drawings, color, anything that will spark ideas, raise questions, or point to connections between facts. Discover how outlines and clusters can be exciting learning tools!

Using References

Questions and Answers

This skill-builder makes using references fun! The game can be played between teams or individuals. It can be used for a brief filler or for an entire class period.

To prepare, first locate duplicate copies of three or four reference books, one copy of each book for each team. It is very important to gather identical books; this ensures that the game will be fair for everyone. Next, develop a list of questions and answers based on your references.

To play, write the first question on the board. One member from each team tackles the question, trying to be the first to locate the correct answer. Appoint a scorekeeper to check answers and keep track of the points earned by each team. The reference books are then passed to the next team member, a new question is written on the board, and play continues. Once your students are familiar with the game, they will enjoy preparing questions and answer cards of their own. For interest, vary the types of references used from day to day. Include dictionaries, your class textbook, almanacs, encyclopedias, instruction manuals, telephone books, atlases, catalogs, and magazines. The winning team is not the one that starts out knowing all the answers; it is the one that knows how to look things up quickly.

Student Reproducibles—Chapter Five

Windmill People—Wasteful attitudes; use with Windmill Thinking sheet.

Windmill Thinking—Wasteful attitudes; students match quotes with personalities. Answers: 1. D, 2. B, 3. G, 4. E, 5. A, 6. F, 7. C. Expand activity by assigning additional dialogue writing. For example, what would Fraidy Freddy say about basketball tryouts?

The Cure for Windmill Thinking—Fun activity; students construct a windmill with a moving blade. Requires scissors, glue, and metal brads.

Protect Your Environment!—Homework distractions. Answers: 1. E; 2. B, D; 3. C; 4. E; 5. A, B, D; 6. D; 7. A; 8. C; 9. B; 10. A; 11. B, D; 12. C. Extend by discussing further common distractions and remedies.

Seven Kinds of Smart—Preference survey; answers will vary. Discuss ways students can use learning preferences to their advantage. For example, a musical person might sing math formulas to herself/himself. A body movement learner could work out an exercise that symbolized different parts of speech. A person strong in numbers, facts, and organization could learn to be a better softball player through studying the science of the pitch.

Climbing Denali—Learning stage survey; answers will vary. Discuss activity by providing specific examples of a person moving through the various stages of learning.

Peking to Paris—Game cards on starting homework, for use with Peking to Paris Gameboard. What other practical suggestions would students add for getting started on an assignment?

Peking to Paris Gameboard—Student gameboard; provide game markers. For enrichment, encourage students to research the details of this history-making automobile race.

The Oyster and the Crab—Student opinion sheet on routine versus variety in study habits; answers will vary. Suggested responses: Advantages to Routine are that it focuses our attention, studying becomes automatic, needed supplies are always at hand. Disadvantages to Routine are that it can be boring, it is too hard to stick with in light of a family's busy schedule, a student might become dependent on a specific place to study. Advantages to Variety are that it is stimulating, it fits students' busy lives, a student learns to study anywhere. Disadvantages to Variety are that it is distracting, a student does not always have needed supplies with him/her, it wastes time in moving supplies from place to place, it is tiring to come up with a new place to study. Follow up with a class vote on the topic. Which do students really think works best for them, routine or variety?

Fiction Action—Student bookmarks on reading tips; duplicate on colored paper and laminate if possible. Apply tips to required novels; students prepare written responses to each step.

Textbook Detective—Mini-mystery to solve; tips for reading nonfiction. The solution to the mystery is that in almost any book, page 202 is printed on the back side of page 201. Use an actual chapter from class text to show how tips apply.

The Secret Keys—Open-ended activity on applying personal interests to studying. Encourage independent research on famous people who turned personal interests into success—Isadora Duncan, R. H. Macy, Hans Christian Andersen, Woodrow Wilson, George Gershwin, Mark Twain, Charles Darwin.

A Note to Home About Homework—Letter on parental involvement with homework. Answers: statements 1, 2, 3, 5, 6, 9, 10 are true; statements 4, 7, 8 are not.

Twelve Tips for Test-Taking—Test strategies. Answers: 1. D, 2. D, 3. A, 4. B, 5. D, 6. A, 7. B, 8. D, 9. B, 10. A, 11. D, 12. D.

The Real Sherlock Holmes—Using reference materials. Answers: 1. E, 2. J, 3. L, 4. H, 5. B, 6. R, 7. O, 8. P, 9. S, 10. D. The real Sherlock Holmes was Dr. Joseph Bell, a surgeon who taught medical students at Edinburgh University. One of his students, Arthur Conan Doyle, remembered his teacher's incredible powers of observation and used them as the basis for the fictional character.

Get Ready to Soar!—Tips for projects and compositions; students fill in blanks, then follow directions to make paper airplane. Answers: 1. begin, plan; 2. time; 3. topic, own; 4. jump, detail; 5. leads, ideas; 6. organize; 7. Reward; 8. writing, take shape; 9. jot, paragraphs; 10. flops, learned.

Windmill People

Wasteful Attitudes

What does a windmill do? It goes around and around, never moving from one spot. What do windmill people do? The very same thing!

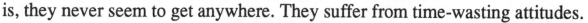

Most of us can easily identify those activities in our lives which waste time, but usually the problem goes deeper—to our attitudes. Here are seven windmill people who stay busy all the time, going around and around. The problem is, they never seem to get anywhere. They suffer from time-wasting attitudes.

Read the descriptions of the characters below and then look at the quotations on the next page. Write each person's letter beside the matching quote.

A. **Juggling Jamie**—Wastes time because he always tries to do too much at once. Jamie is interested in hundreds of things, but gets nothing done.

B. **Yes-Yes Yolanda**—Never says no to anything! Yolanda does everything with everybody, so she never has time to get her work done.

C. **In-a-Minute Mike**—His problem is procrastination. He always means to get his work done, but he'll get around to it "in a minute."

D. **Whining Wynona**—Complain, fret, whine. Wynona spends so much time complaining, she never has time to actually work.

E. **Fraidy Freddy**—Poor Freddy is so afraid of failing, he does not try at all. Why bring books home if you know you cannot do the work?

F. **Just-Right Justine**—She drives herself (and everyone else) crazy trying to be perfect. Her reports always need a little more work so they can be just right.

G. **Impatient Paco**—Paco lives in the fast lane. He is always in a hurry, and when things do not go right on the first try, he blows up. Paco starts lots of assignments, but wastes time because he quits part-way through.

Windmill Thinking

Wasteful Attitudes

Read each quotation and decide which windmill person is the speaker. Write the person's letter beside the quote.

_____1. "Oh, dear, I just don't know if I'm doing this math right. My teacher is so hard. Rats, my pencil broke. Now I'll have to hunt up a new one—if I can find it. I never have pencils when I need them. Nobody ever buys pencils for me around here."

_____2. "Go skating after school? Sure! Yes, I promised Jill I would help her make posters for the club meeting, but I can do both. Yes, I still have to finish my science project, but I'll squeeze it in somehow."

_____3. "This first problem is too hard. I give up! I'll try my language assignment. H-m-m-m, I'm supposed to find the direct object. I know it's one of these words. Is a direct object a verb or an adjective? Oh, just forget it! I'll do my social studies."

_____4. "I'll just stick all these books in my locker for the night. I don't understand any of the stuff, anyway. I couldn't do any good anyway, so why waste time trying?"

_____5. "First, I have to stop at the library and read some books for my science project and pick out a novel for my book report. And on the way, I'll get posterboard for my campaign posters for school secretary and some graph paper for that extra-credit math assignment. Then I'll come home, read the novel, write the book report, and start outlining my science project—*after* I've made my campaign posters."

_____6. "This report was due two days ago, but I still don't have my last two pages right. I just can't get the words to say exactly what I want them to say."

_____7. "As soon as the Bulls make a point, I'll turn off the TV and start my homework. Rats, the Celtics have the ball. As soon as the Bulls get the ball back, I'll get busy on my work."

The Cure for Windmill Thinking

Wasteful Attitudes

Here is a fun way to tackle your own windmill thinking!

1. On Figure A, complete the sentence under the happy face.
2. On Figure B, finish the sentence beneath the sad face.
3. Cut out the figures and glue the blank sides together.
4. Now cut out the windmill blade. Place it on the + on Figure A (the side with the happy face) and attach with a metal brad.

If you have followed directions carefully, one side of your windmill will show what you look like when you have time-wasting attitudes. Turn the windmill over and you will see yourself walking away from the problem!

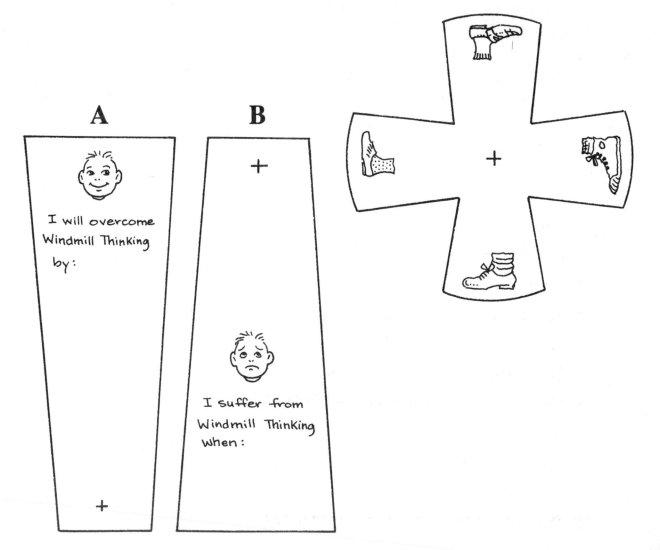

A

I will overcome
Windmill Thinking
by:

+

B

+

I suffer from
Windmill Thinking
when:

Protect Your Environment!

Study Pollution

Distractions while you are doing your homework are just like empty cans and bottles on a beautiful beach. We call it all pollution! What is polluting your study time? Here are five common student complaints about study time. Listed below are some easy solutions. Write the complaint letter next to a matching solution. (Some solutions may help more than one problem.)

A. "Every time I sit down to study, one of my friends calls me on the phone."

B. "Even though they play in another room, my little brothers make as much noise as a herd of hyenas!"

C. "I have a hard time keeping my eyes off interesting things in my room. I even waste time staring out my window!"

D. "My mother always comes into my room while I am studying. She says she is just checking, but she always starts talking about other things, and it gets me off-track."

E. "I like to study on my bed because it is comfortable. But I often end up falling asleep."

_____ 1. Always study at a desk or table.

_____ 2. Wear earplugs.

_____ 3. Close the blinds.

_____ 4. Get a chair with a firm seat and back.

_____ 5. Enlist your family's help in maintaining a quiet study time.

_____ 6. Post a "Do Not Disturb" sign.

_____ 7. Use a phone answering machine.

_____ 8. Turn your desk away from the window.

_____ 9. Play soft background music.

_____10. Have a family member take your phone messages.

_____11. Close your door.

_____12. Put away enticing books and magazines.

Seven Kinds of Smart

Intelligence

The more we learn about the human brain, the more we discover that intelligence comes in many forms. Scientists now say there are as many as seven different kinds of intelligence. In how many of the seven areas are you smart? Check the sentences below that are especially true for you.

_____ 1. You like to fix things.
_____ 2. You frequently listen to music.
_____ 3. You are happiest spending time with friends.
_____ 4. You can usually spot a misspelled word.
_____ 5. You are curious and frequently ask "why" questions.
_____ 6. You doodle all the time.
_____ 7. You can imagine yourself in many different situations.
_____ 8. You keep your room or desk organized.
_____ 9. You like to meet new people.
_____ 10. You like to tell stories.
_____ 11. You are physically very coordinated.
_____ 12. You feel bad when a friend is in trouble.
_____ 13. You like to read science magazines.
_____ 14. You think about your feelings frequently.
_____ 15. You like to sing.
_____ 16. You give good directions to places.
_____ 17. You keep a diary or a journal.
_____ 18. You are often aware of the sounds around you.
_____ 19. You like maps.
_____ 20. You are a good dancer.
_____ 21. You are good at remembering jokes and poetry.

Now look at the sentences you checked.

4, 17, 21	=	Intelligence of words
5, 13, 8	=	Intelligence of numbers, facts, and organization
2, 15, 18	=	Intelligence of music
6, 16, 19	=	Intelligence of places, locations, and shapes
1, 11, 20	=	Intelligence of body movement
7, 14, 10	=	Intelligence of understanding yourself
3, 9, 12	=	Intelligence of understanding other people

If you checked all three sentences in a category you are strong in that area. Once you know your best areas, you can make them work for you. How can you use a strength to help you learn in various subjects?

Climbing Denali

Levels of Learning

Mount McKinley, in south-central Alaska, is the highest peak in North America. The Indian name for the mountain is *Denali*, which means "The Great One." Only great learners get to climb to the top of The Great One! Test your climbing ability with the questions below. For each of your school subjects, decide which level you are on. What do you need to do to move higher up Denali?

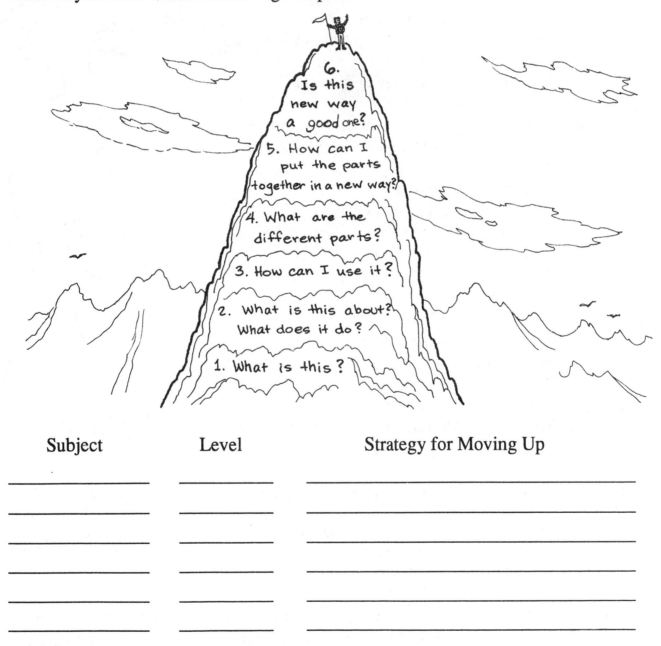

Subject	Level	Strategy for Moving Up
_____	_____	_____
_____	_____	_____
_____	_____	_____
_____	_____	_____
_____	_____	_____

Peking to Paris

Getting Started

In 1907, most people believed that the car would never replace the horse. A French newspaper, *Le Matin*, proposed an almost impossible test—a race from Peking, China, to Paris, France, a distance of over 8,000 miles. For most of the way there were no roads, only desert paths, forest trails, and mountain passes. If anyone could complete the trip, it would guarantee the future of the automobile.

Motorists from around the world considered entering the race, but only five cars pulled up to the starting line. How did they have the courage to start on such an impossible challenge? The very same way you convince yourself to start on your homework! Cut out the START cards below and use them with the "Peking to Paris Gameboard."

On August 10, 1907, Italian Prince Scipione Borghese and his crew sputtered into Paris, 61 days after leaving Peking. To this day, the race remains one of the most sensational automotive achievements in history.

START CARDS

You start by getting your tools and supplies ready.	You start with a plan in mind.	You start with something you like.	You start with the most difficult job. It makes the rest seem easy.
You start early, before you get tired.	You start with a stopping time in mind. You try to finish on time.	You start with your results in mind.	You start with a small, do-able job.
You start by thinking of a reward for finishing the job.	You start in plenty of time. You do not wait until the last minute.	You start by removing roadblocks and distractions.	You start by putting blinders on. All you see is the task in front of you.

Peking to Paris Gameboard

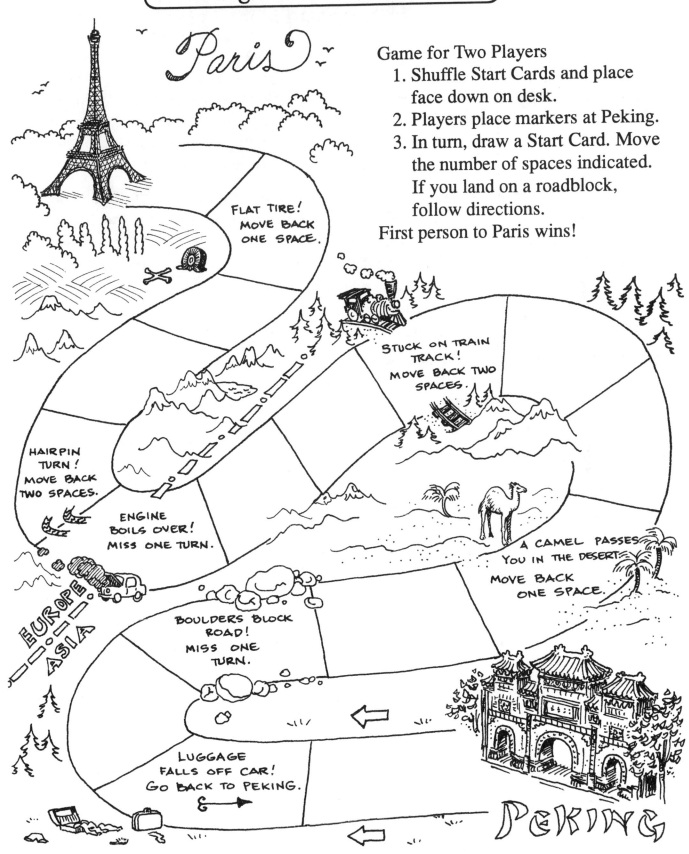

Paris

Game for Two Players
1. Shuffle Start Cards and place face down on desk.
2. Players place markers at Peking.
3. In turn, draw a Start Card. Move the number of spaces indicated. If you land on a roadblock, follow directions.
First person to Paris wins!

FLAT TIRE!
MOVE BACK ONE SPACE.

STUCK ON TRAIN TRACK!
MOVE BACK TWO SPACES.

HAIRPIN TURN!
MOVE BACK TWO SPACES.

ENGINE BOILS OVER!
MISS ONE TURN.

A CAMEL PASSES YOU IN THE DESERT.
MOVE BACK ONE SPACE.

EUROPE
ASIA

BOULDERS BLOCK ROAD!
MISS ONE TURN.

LUGGAGE FALLS OFF CAR!
GO BACK TO PEKING.

PEKING

The Oyster and the Crab
Routine Vs. Variety

The creatures that live in the salt marsh fall into two categories—those like the oyster, who stay in one spot and live by a routine, and those like the crab, who prefer to roam the sea, finding food in a new place every day. When it comes to study preferences, are you an oyster or a crab? Read to find out.

The oyster, lover of routine, likes to study in the same place at the same time every day. She knows her supplies are right there when she needs them. When the oyster follows her personal routine, her mind automatically settles down to study.

The crab likes variety when he studies. He can work at home, outside, at the library, or in the car, because his family is always on the go. The crab finds this change of scene interesting and does not mind carrying his supplies with him.

Now list three advantages and three disadvantages of each study preference.

	Routine	Variety
Advantages:	1._____	1._____
	2._____	2._____
	3._____	3._____
Disadvantages:	1._____	1._____
	2._____	2._____
	3._____	3._____

Complete this statement: I am a(n) oyster/crab. Routine/Variety is the best way for me to study because _____

_____

_____

Fiction Action

Reading Fiction

Mount these bookmarks on heavy paper, cut them out, and keep them in the novels you are reading. The tips will help you enjoy real Fiction Action!

How to REALLY read a novel!

Beforehand:

- Skim for difficult words. Look them up.

- Understand the setting.

- Figure out the general theme.

During:

- Ask "Who? What? Where? Why?"

- Ask "What do I think will happen next?"

- Ask "What would happen if. . .?"

GREAT WAYS to enjoy required novels!

- Listen to a cassette tape of the book after you have read it.

- Watch a video version and compare it to the novel. (The book is usually better!)

- Read the dialogue out loud with a friend.

- Read about the author. Why did he or she write the novel?

Textbook Detective
Reading Nonfiction

See if you can solve this mystery.

Slimy Jones, a kid of questionable character, walked into class one day waving a $100 bill. "Hey, everybody! Look what I just found!" Slimy announced.

The teacher, Mrs. Barton, asked where he had found the money.

"It was in my science textbook," Slimy said. "Stuck in between pages 201 and 202."

Sarah Rupert, ace textbook detective, quickly spoke up. "That is impossible, Mrs. Barton. Slimy is not telling us the truth."

How does Sarah know that Slimy is lying?

You may not know the answer to the mystery above, but you too can be an ace textbook detective. Here are Sarah Rupert's rules for tackling an assigned chapter.

1. Preview the chapter headings and captions, the introduction, and the summary.

2. Read over the questions at the end of the chapter.

3. Read the chapter carefully. Nonfiction usually must be read more slowly than fiction.

4. Now go back and answer the questions, looking back through the book when necessary.

5. NEVER try to answer the questions by simply flipping through the pages. If you do not read the chapter carefully, you will miss important facts and ideas.

Now, back to the mystery! Examine a textbook carefully to discover what Sarah Rupert knows.

The Secret Keys

Personal Involvement

In your possession right now are secret keys that will open the door to success in almost any school subject. These keys are your special interests, those things that fascinate you in your free time.

How do these keys work? Here is an example: If you hate social studies, but you love to cook, find some recipes to prepare from the country your class is studying. What can you discover about the culture from its food? Before you know it, you will have learned about agriculture, racial and ethnic groups, religion, trade, income—all because of your secret key, an interest in cooking.

What are your special interests? Write them in the key boxes below. Then list ways your interests can help you enjoy learning in each subject area.

Special Interests			
Math			
Science			
Social Studies			
Language Arts			
Foreign Language			

A Note to Home About Homework
Parent Letter

Dear Family,

Research shows that you are your child's best teacher when it comes to homework! Even families who know very little about a subject can make a big difference—all it takes is a caring attitude and some helpful guidance. See how you score on the quiz below. Check each statement that is true.

_____ 1. A caring family limits the number of after-school activities so the child has enough time to do homework.

_____ 2. A caring family tries to provide a quiet atmosphere during study time.

_____ 3. A caring family asks to see assignments and test papers on a regular basis.

_____ 4. A caring family gives the child all the answers to a tough assignment.

_____ 5. A caring family sits with the child and helps him/her think through a tough assignment.

_____ 6. A caring family knows that the child needs a healthy balance of homework and relaxation.

_____ 7. A caring family finishes an assignment for the child who did not budget his/her time properly.

_____ 8. A caring family expects homework perfection.

_____ 9. A caring family expects homework progress.

_____ 10. A caring family takes up concerns with the teacher instead of complaining at home.

Give yourself an A+ if you made seven checks! Thanks for all the support and guidance you give your child. Your feelings about homework greatly influence your child's performance. Keep up the good work!

Twelve Tips for Test-Taking

Test-Taking

How much do you know about taking a test? Here are the 12 test strategies that every student should remember. Label each one:

          B - Before you take the test.
          D - During the test.
          A - After you take the test.

_____ 1. Read the directions slowly and carefully.

_____ 2. Check for mistakes in math after you have finished.

_____ 3. Go back and learn the information you missed on the test.

_____ 4. Do not cram, but study in short doses every day.

_____ 5. Save the long and difficult questions for last.

_____ 6. File the test so you can review it later for final exams.

_____ 7. Look in the mirror and say, "I studied hard. I am prepared. I know I am going to do my very best."

_____ 8. Do the quick and easy questions first.

_____ 9. Get enough sleep and a healthy breakfast.

_____ 10. Analyze the mistakes you made on the test.

_____ 11. Reread the questions and answers after you have finished.

_____ 12. Find the action called for in the directions and circle it.

The Real Sherlock Holmes

Using References

Books are not the only source of good information. There are many other resources available in your community. When you research a topic, be like Sherlock Holmes and track down facts from the best source possible.

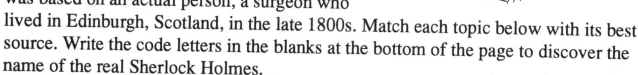

The character of the famous fictional detective was based on an actual person, a surgeon who lived in Edinburgh, Scotland, in the late 1800s. Match each topic below with its best source. Write the code letters in the blanks at the bottom of the page to discover the name of the real Sherlock Holmes.

J. Dictionary   L. Thesaurus   H. Encyclopedia
S. Local industries   D. Health department E. Magazine
O. Atlas   B. Local newspaper P. Almanac
               R. Local government

_____ 1. To learn about the designs of the newest boats on the market.

_____ 2. To find out how to divide the word *hippopotamus* into syllables.

_____ 3. To find six synonyms for the word *brave*.

_____ 4. To read a brief summary of Theodore Roosevelt's life.

_____ 5. To learn some background information on the candidates who are running for mayor.

_____ 6. To find out what the local regulations are for building a garage on your property.

_____ 7. To find out the distance between St. Joseph, Missouri, and Chicago, Illinois.

_____ 8. To find out the names of last year's Nobel Prize winners.

_____ 9. To learn if the factories in your area are hiring workers.

_____ 10. To learn which diseases are the biggest problems in your town.

___ ___   ___ ___ ___ ___ ___ ___   ___ ___ ___ ___
10 6   2 7 9 1 8 4   5 1 3 3

Name_____

Get Ready to Soar!

Projects and Compositions

Independent assignments are your chance to explore new horizons on your own. Writing a composition or working on a project is like piloting a plane. Fuel up with facts and figures; then soar where no one else has gone before! Use the Word Bank to fill in the blanks below; then follow the directions to make a loop-the-loop airplane.

1. Before you _____ a big project, make a step-by-step _____ of action.

2. Plan on plenty of _____ to complete each step.

3. Choose your own _____ , not one that your friend likes. Make your project your very _____.

4. Once you have a plan, _____ in! You do not have to know every _____ at the beginning.

5. Go where your project _____ you. As you read and think, your _____ may change.

6. Talk over your ideas with someone. Saying things out loud helps you _____ your thoughts.

7. _____ yourself for every step you complete. It will recharge your energy!

8. Before you begin _____ , let your ideas _____ in your head for a while. Think about them when you take a shower or before you go to sleep.

9. To ease into writing, _____ down good phrases and sentences. Then build _____ around them.

10. If your project _____, do not panic. Write exactly what happened and what you _____. The world has gained much knowledge through flops!

Word Bank

begin
take shape
detail
flops
ideas
jot
jump
learned
organize
own
paragraphs
plan
reward
leads
time
topic
writing

Airplane Directions

1. Fold up the long edge of the paper eight times.
2. Fold paper in half crosswise; cut along cut line.
3. Open paper. Fold wing tips up.
4. Turn paper over. Fold small rear wing tips down.

FOLD

CUT LINE

Meeting Extracurricular Needs

Shinkeishitsu

Do your students suffer from *shinkeishitsu*? That means "nervous temperament" in Japanese, and it describes the physical discomfort that children and adults alike feel when they have too much to do. Both Japan and the United States have developed a cultural problem of "busyness;" even our preschoolers feel the push to achieve and excel.

With your students, make a list of the ways that we push children today. Consider the toys and products we buy for them, the lessons, sports, and activities we schedule, and the messages we send through the media. Here are a few starters:

Toys:	dolls with mature figures, makeup kits for little girls, video games that feature adult violence
Products:	video programs that teach early reading and foreign language, exercise videos
Activities:	toddler soccer teams, infant swimming lessons, toddler music lessons, baby beauty pageants, seventh grade SATs, early dating

While excellence is unquestionably a worthy pursuit, it can be carried to the extreme. Much of the disorder in our students' private lives is there simply because they and their families have taken on too much. Together, examine these symptoms:

I know I have *shinkeishitsu* if . . .
- I have trouble relaxing even when my work is finished.
- I do not enjoy spending a quiet evening at home.
- I am not satisfied, no matter what I achieve.
- I worry constantly about things I cannot change.
- I am not happy unless I am super-successful.

The cure for *shinkeishitsu* is moderation, that balanced, happy-medium state that is so hard for some of us to find. Encourage your students to take a look at their after-school schedules. Sometimes eliminating just one extra activity is a huge step toward making life manageable.

Mind Power

The quest for moderation begins in the mind, with self-discipline. Linda and Richard Eyre, authors and family advocates, recommend these four simple mottoes that will help students in their quest for order:

Mind over Matter. (I am too smart to be defeated by clutter!)
Mind over Mattress. (My desire to get up on time is stronger than my desire to sleep.)
Mind over Muscle. (My mind will overrule the complaints of my lazy body.)
Mind over Menu. (My appetite will not defeat my mind!)

Instruct students to record the number of times in one day that they apply each of these slogans. What was the situation? Did the slogan help?

Red Light-Green Light

"My biggest problem is my family. I set goals for myself and make great plans with my friends—and then my family messes everything up!"

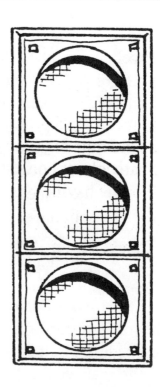

By middle school, most students have outgrown childhood's idealistic love of family. In a heartbeat, they can name a thousand and one imperfections of their parents and siblings. As you discuss the importance of time management at home, point out that the ability to accept family members *as they are* is a sign of maturity. A child *reacts* to those around him; a young adult *tries to understand*. Use the activity Red Light-Green Light to illustrate the difference.

With the class, list on the chalkboard some typical family situations that can cause discord. The easy part is first—to come up with a Red Light response for each situation, a childish reaction that is angry and unproductive. Then direct students to think of more understanding Green Light reactions, ones in which they look for compromise or common ground.

	Red Light	Green Light
Parent asks you to clean your room just as you are going out to play ball.	Explode and slam door. Clean room and pout. Run out without listening.	Agree on a time later for cleaning the room. Work fast so you still have time to play.
Your younger brother is bugging you—again!	Call him names and send him away crying.	Get him busy doing something he likes so you can get away.
The family is going to visit your elderly grandmother in a nursing home. You hate going there.	Refuse to go. Go, but cry and complain all the way. Be rude when you get there.	Remember that your dad loves your grandmother. This is not easy for him either. Realize that some day you might be in the same situation.

Here are some good guidelines for making family life more manageable.

- Remember, no one has the perfect family.
- Spend time together doing something you all can enjoy.
- Share jobs at home.
- Work at having times of good communication (listening and talking).

Time at home does not have to be chaos; even a middle schooler can help his/her family find common ground.

Goal Coach

Here is a radical approach to handling family criticism—teach your students to ask for it!

Defuse the hurt of negative comments from home with a new point of view. Family criticism is like coaching. It comes from people who want you on their team, who are trying to help you improve. Critical remarks are only observations; they are not judgments. Extend the coaching comparison by encouraging students to select a family member as a personal goal coach. This individual is someone who will help evaluate progress. It may be a kind, sympathetic person, or it may be the most critical individual in the family. Use the letter below as a model for notes students write to their goal coaches:

Dear _____,

As you may know, I have set some goals for myself at school and here at home. It will require dedication and hard work if I am to reach those goals. As I begin, I know there will be times when I fail or get discouraged. That is why I am asking you to be my goal coach. Will you watch and encourage me when I need it most?

Even though I have trouble accepting criticism, I need it, so *I will ask for it* on a regular basis. Will you save your advice and criticism until I come to you? I would like to plan on a regular time for this, when you can tell me how I am doing.

Having my own personal coach will be great! Thanks for caring enough to help me reach my goals.

Love,

_____

The beauty of this note is that it works on both the sender and the receiver. It puts responsibility for progress on the student, and it reminds the family member to offer criticism with care.

Junk Jamboree

As every yard sale shopper knows, "One man's trash is another man's treasure." Turn student bedroom clutter into classroom gold with a Junk Jamboree.

First, send students home on a mission—to seek and destroy messy rooms. As proof of their success, they are to bring back to school three junk items that they uncovered in the cleanup. These items should be small enough to fit in their book bags, and of no possible use to anyone. Examples: a ticket stub, a used-up assignment pad, a pen cap, a candy wrapper, a broken shoelace.

Now decide how you will incorporate these cast-off items into your lesson plans. It is amazing what you can do with a little junk!

- In math class, redistribute the items and assign students the task of writing word problems about them.

- What would an archeologist of the future learn about our civilization if she unearthed these items? Prepare a junk time capsule to leave in your school's archives.

- Use the collection of items to inspire creative writing. Mary Norton, an English author, based her popular series of children's novels, *The Borrowers*, on junk. Suggest that students write wacky, Dr.-Seuss-style poetry, mysteries with junk clues, or lyrics to songs like, "I've Got the Messy-Room Blues."

- Discuss scientific ways to classify the items—by size, by use, by composition, by color.

- Divide students into groups for some cooperative creativity, inventing strange new uses for the junk or assembling recycled works of art.

Your plans for a Junk Jamboree could grow to include a school-wide emphasis on litter, including a recycled art show, a yard sale, an invention convention using cast-off materials, taping public service announcements for local media, a poster campaign, a clean sweep of the school grounds.

The Cleanie Genie

Read this short story out loud to your students and direct them to write down the Cleanie Genie's ten tips for cleaning up a messy room. (They are each indicated by a star in the story text.)

The Cleanie Genie

"Rats, might as well get started!" Ray heaved a sigh and walked over to the shelf that held dozens of dusty trophies. Ray was a good athlete and had been collecting trophies ever since he started playing sports in kindergarten. A good athlete, definitely, but a lousy cleaner. Ray's mother had just grounded him until his room was spotless.

"Hey, I don't remember this trophy! I wonder what I got it for?" Ray reached through the assorted trophies to pick up a small one on the back row. He squinted to read the tarnished letters engraved on the cup, "For Ray: Rub if you ne . . ." The rest of the letters were blackened with age. Ray grabbed his shirt tail and tried to polish the trophy.

P-f-f-f-t! Out of the top of the trophy cup popped a tiny bird-like old woman with a dust cloth in one hand and a bottle of cleaner in the other. "Well, it's about time, young man! That's all I can say, it's about time! I've been waiting for years for you to wake up to see the junk pile you're living in!" The little old woman waved the dust cloth under Ray's nose.

"W-h-h-o-o-o are you?" stammered Ray.

"Me? I'm the Cleanie Genie. You summoned me when you wiped the dust off my trophy. But come on, Ray, time's a-wastin'. Make that dust cloth move. Hup-two-three-four!"

"Wait a minute," Ray said, thinking hard. "You're a genie, right? That means you're magic. And if you're magic, you can wave your wand and make my room clean instantly! All right, I can still make that soccer game this afternoon! Come on, Genie, what's the magic word—abracadabra? Sha-zam? Bippity-boppity-boo? Supercalifrag... ?"

The tiny genie silenced Ray with a glare from her beady little eyes. "Where have you been, Ray? It's the '90s. We magic folk are liberated now. No more 'Your wish is my command' stuff. No, Ray, I'm here to supervise! For starts,

(*) don't wait so long to clean next time. When the problem is this big, it's UNMANAGEABLE!" And with that, the Cleanie Genie pushed the dirty clothes off Ray's bed and plopped down.

For the next three hours, Ray worked like a dog. The genie made him open every drawer. "You call that stuff odds and ends? Well if it's so odd, get rid of it! (*) Eliminate clutter, Ray, eliminate clutter!"

Ray tried working back and forth, cleaning his dresser for a while and then moving over to his desk, but the genie set him straight. (*) " Work like a football player, Ray. Tackle just one thing at a time."

Next, Ray started tossing his sports equipment in the corner of his room. Genie wagged her finger. (*) "No-no-no! A place for everything, and everything in its place!"

Ray thought he was in pretty good shape, but the little old lady taught him some new moves, like (*) putting things he rarely used high up on closet shelves. "Keep frequently used items close by, dearie," she said.

When Ray wanted to take a break, the Cleanie Genie wouldn't hear of it. "Once you get started, don't stop until you're through!" she shrieked. "Why drag out the job?"

As Ray straightened up his school notebooks, he saw he was running out of notebook paper. The genie shoved a pencil and pad into his hand. (*) "L is for *list*, Ray. Keep a list of the things you need for your next shopping trip!"

The place was starting to look like a room and not a junk pile. Genie glanced at her watch. "Ray! (*) If you can make your bed in the next three minutes, you will have set a new world's record! Come on, Ray, you can do it! Beat the clock!" Ray tackled the bed, a whirl of clean sheets and blankets. Two and a half minutes later, he collapsed on the floor beside the Cleanie Genie.

She patted his hand sweetly. "Very good, my dear. I have to be off now, but I'm going to give you two more pieces of advice. See how nice your room looks now? (*) To keep it that way, do a little cleaning every day, and (*) if the mood strikes you to clean, DO IT!"

With fizzle of smoke and the strong odor of pine cleaner, the genie was gone. From then on, whenever Ray tackled his room, he looked for the little trophy. And no matter how thoroughly he cleaned, he could never find it. But it didn't matter; the genie had done her work well. Ray's room stayed clean.

The Kimono Secret

Most students with a clutter problem clean only when they have to, because a parent or teacher requires it. Since the appearance of tidiness is what counts, they concentrate on those things that show. But what if they tackled a hidden area of disorder? What if they did it just for their own personal benefit, and not because they had to? Traditional Japanese culture considered private order and beauty the greatest luxury of all. It is interesting to note that the severe, plain kimonos worn by men were lined with gorgeous bright fabrics on the inside. These beautiful linings never showed. They were strictly for the enjoyment of the wearer.

Use a three-minute art activity to discuss the private pleasure that comes from a clean drawer or an organized closet, even if no one else ever sees it. Ahead of time, cut out one-inch squares of colored paper, enough for three squares per student. Distribute the squares, along with blank index cards and glue. Show the class how to make a kimono shape on the card, using two squares for sleeves and one for the body. Students then draw in feet and faces. On the bottom of the card, students complete this statement:

"The secret of the kimono is its hidden beauty. I resolve to organize my _____ because I need hidden beauty, too. This is something I will do just for me. It matters, even if no one else ever notices."

Help Wanted

Chores at home are a perennial source of conflict between parents and middle schoolers. In most cases, differing expectations are the root of the problem. Present a new perspective with this activity in which students see their parents as employers and themselves as employees.

First, distribute samples of actual want ads from your local newspaper. Do a survey of the range of duties and benefits offered. Discuss the concept of a benefit package; a job applicant often bases his/her decision not on salary alone, but also on the benefits offered. Next, hand out the job description form below. What do students think of the benefit package provided by this employer? What kind of work would deserve such generous benefits? Soon someone will realize that these benefits apply to most students living at home. For all the perks that families offer, they ask very little in return. Direct your students to complete the job description form, personalizing it with their own list of required duties at home.

JOB DESCRIPTION FORM

HELP WANTED: _____

_____

_____

_____

SALARY:_____

BENEFITS TO INCLUDE: Paid vacation, total health care and insurance, unlimited sick leave, uniforms, chauffeur-driven car, gourmet meals, tastefully furnished room. Higher educational funding available to qualified applicants.

Attitudes About Money

Dollars and Sense

Kick off a discussion of healthy attitudes about money with a quick trivia quiz. See if students know as much about the subject as they think they do. No peeking in wallets during the quiz!

Whose face is on each of these bills?

$1	(George Washington)
$5	(Abraham Lincoln)
$10	(Alexander Hamilton)
$20	(Andrew Jackson)

Whose face is on each of these coins?

penny	(Abraham Lincoln)
nickel	(Thomas Jefferson)
dime	(Franklin D. Roosevelt)
quarter	(George Washington)
half dollar	(John F. Kennedy)

What is the Latin motto stamped on all U. S. coins?
What does it mean?
(*E Pluribus Unum* - Out of many, one.)

If your class is typical, students will be able to answer only about half of these simple questions correctly. Given our culture's preoccupation with money, why do we know so little about it? Is our ignorance due in part to the fact that we live in one of the richest countries in the world? Here are some chilling facts:

- At this moment, one fourth of the world's children are going to bed hungry.
- Six percent of the world's population spends 40 percent of the money.
- The United Nations estimates that over 300 million of the world's people cannot find employment.
- In some developing countries today, the average wage for a day of hard physical labor is $1.50.

Our concerns about money pale in comparison.

The typical middle schooler's attitude toward money seems to be, "Spend, spend, spend!" Our culture has done a superb job of capturing their thoughts and pocketbooks! But does all this spending truly satisfy? Discuss the endless cycle of spending and dissatisfaction in which many people find themselves. Present the diagram below and direct students to write about their own experiences with this money trap. Encourage the class to look for examples of printed ads, jingles, slogans, and attitudes that show how our culture pushes us into the cycle.

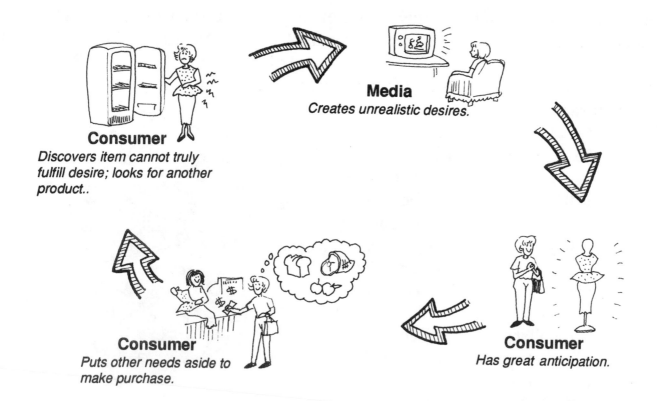

Media
Creates unrealistic desires.

Consumer
Discovers item cannot truly fulfill desire; looks for another product..

Consumer
Puts other needs aside to make purchase.

Consumer
Has great anticipation.

Student Reproducibles—Chapter Six

Juggling Act—Extracurricular goal sheet; answers will vary. For enrichment, locate a copy of *Juggling for the Complete Klutz* by John Cassidy and B. C. Rimbeaux. Provide old tennis balls, bean bags, or wads of paper and schedule a classroom juggling lesson to make your point about juggling too many extra goals.

Branching Out—Survey sheet on new activities; answers will vary. Extend by giving students the assignment to try one new activity per month and report on their experiences. Invite people with unusual careers or hobbies to share them with your class.

The Mess Test—Humorous definitions. Compile students' own illustrated definitions into a notebook for classroom sharing.

My Space: My World—Student evaluation of personal space at home; answers will vary. Encourage students to value and care for their rooms. Extend by assigning visual mock-ups of the perfect room, using three-dimensional models or pictures clipped from magazines.

Family Responsibility Contract—Student-parent form for listing household chores; answers will vary.

Monthly Student Budget Sheet—Form for examining personal income and spending; answers will vary.

Juggling Act

Limiting Extracurricular Goals

Enrico Rastelli, an Italian circus performer of the 1940s, is considered to be the best juggler of all time. He could juggle 11 objects at once, but it took 12 hours of practice every day to maintain his skill.

Very few of us can juggle more than three priorities at one time. As a young person, two of those priorities have been decided for you—school requirements and family requirements. The third priority is up to you—a sport, a hobby, lessons. On the diagram below, list just one goal per day for each of your three priorities. If you are tempted to set more than one goal per day just remember. You're not Enrico Rastelli!

School

Mon. _____

Tues. _____

Wed. _____

Thurs. _____

Fri. _____

Family

Mon. _____

Tues. _____

Wed. _____

Thurs. _____

Fri. _____

Self

Mon. _____

Tues. _____

Wed. _____

Thurs. _____

Fri. _____

Branching Out

Trying New Things

A strong healthy tree develops new growth on all sides. How about you? Are you branching out to explore interesting new activities? Complete each section below.

List your current hobbies and activities here. Put an X in each category that applies.

Hobbies	Independent Activity	Group Activity	Activity to Benefit Others	Activity to Benefit Self	Musical Activity	Physical Activity	Artistic Activity	Mental Activity
1.								
2.								
3.								
4.								

Look at your Xs. How balanced are you? Where are you weak? What can you do to branch out?

_____

_____

_____

_____

_____

Look over this list of activities. Check the ones you have tried. Circle the ones you would like to try. Are you brave enough to branch out?

computers   reading
soccer   ceramics
woodworking   ice skating
sewing   track
chess   baseball
scouting   stamps
skiing   Ping-Pong
school clubs   singing
martial arts   cooking
crafts   volleyball
roller-skating   tennis
coins   volunteering
auto mechanics   sculpting
acting   quilting
kites   models
puppets   knitting
church group   4-H
surfing   hockey
gymnastics   cheerleading
drawing   music
bowling   twirling
writing   dancing
swimming   OTHER:
wrestling
football   _____
painting   _____
civic clubs   _____
ham radio   _____
boating

Name_____

The Mess Test

Handling Clutter

Students and parents agree, a messy room is the number one reason for disagreements at home. Just for fun, see if you know the "messy" definitions of the words below.

zero
a. a state of nothingness.
b. the number of minutes you spend straightening your room each week.

avalanche
a. a large mass of snow that slides down a mountain.
b. what falls out of your closet when you open the door.

junk
a. items of little value.
b. everything in your desk drawer.

black hole
a. a dead star.
b. the corner of your room where dirty socks seem to disappear.

chaos
a. the original unformed state of the universe.
b. your room.

oxygen
a. a colorless, odorless gas.
b. what you need when you pick up your dirty clothes piled in the bathroom.

pack rat
a. a large bushy-tailed rodent from western North America that stores food and other items.
b. you.

perpetual motion machine
a. a device that can work continually without stopping. Not even the most brilliant scientists in the world have succeeded in making one.
b. what your parents think you are.

Now write some "messy" definitions of your own! Use the words below or any others you choose.

tidal wave	mold	vacuum	dust
pigsty	heart attack	Grand Canyon	mirage
national disaster	cobweb	sponge	recycle

My Space: My World

Managing Bedroom Clutter

Whether you have a huge room all to yourself or share a tiny corner with brothers or sisters, your space is your personal world. A messy room is depressing; it slows you down when you cannot find what you need. A clean organized room is an instant boost. Check the statements below that apply to your space at home.

_____ My space is a good place to rest and recharge.
_____ My space is a spot where I dream and plan.
_____ My space is my shelter from the world.
_____ My space is an original work of art—it expresses my personality.
_____ My space is well-organized for my activities and belongings.

To be just right, your space does not necessarily need designer sheets or the latest in sound equipment. It does need to meet your personal requirements for privacy, for comfort, for convenience, for enjoyment. Complete the statements below.

The worst thing about my space is _____
_____
_____
_____

The best thing about my space is _____
_____
_____
_____

If I could have any kind of room I wanted, I would_____
_____
_____
_____
_____

Family Responsibility Contract

Chores

Use this sheet to think about the ways you can help out at home. After you have written down your ideas, discuss them with your family.

Jobs I will do just because I am a member of this family

_____

_____

_____

Jobs I will do to earn privileges or spending money

_____

_____

_____

Extra work I can do if I need money for a special purpose

_____

_____

Your commitment to your family:

I agree to do the jobs listed above willingly and without being nagged. Doing these chores will help my family, and I will learn to be a responsible worker. Best of all, I will earn something on my own!

_____
Your signature

_____
A family member's signature

_____
Date

Name_____

Monthly Student Budget Sheet

Spending and Saving

It is never too early to learn how to manage your money, even if it is only lawn-mowing and baby-sitting money. Use this form to organize your money and to plan how to use it.

Income

    Allowance _____

    Amount _____
    earned _____

            _____

            _____

    Other _____

Total spendable income _____

Expenses

    School lunches _____

    Snacks _____

    Clothing _____

    School Supplies _____

    Club dues,
    offerings, etc. _____

    Transportation _____

    Recreation/
    Entertainment _____

    Other _____

Total expenses _____

Amount to
save monthly _____

Future Purchases

    Item: _____

    Cost: _____

    How to Pay for: _____

    _____

    _____

    Item: _____

    Cost: _____

    How to Pay for: _____

    _____

    _____

    Item: _____

    Cost: _____

    How to Pay for: _____

    _____

    _____

Major Savings Goal

    Purpose: _____

    Amount: _____

    How to achieve goal: _____

    _____

    _____

The Payoff: Enjoying Order

Work and Play

The goal of most students in implementing time management techniques is to finish their schoolwork quickly and gain more time for play. That is a compartmentalized approach to living. Our goal as lifelong learners should be to tear down the wall between work and play.

Tell students about the role that play had in the invention of the telescope. An eyeglass lens grinder named Hans Lippershey lived in Middleburg, Holland, around 1600. As he was taking a break from his work one day, two neighborhood boys entered the workshop and began playing with the lenses there. One of the boys stacked a thick convex lens on top of a concave one and held the two together up to his eye. The church steeple on the other side of the village jumped at him through the lenses. It scared the boy so, he almost dropped the two pieces of glass. His friend repeated the experiment and had the same experience. The steeple that was a good distance away appeared to be right next door. The boys rushed to show Hans Lippershey, and they spent the rest of the day playing with different pieces of glass. Later, the lens grinder devised a tube to hold both lenses, and the first telescope was born.

The significant question is, was Hans Lippershey working or playing? Many other inventions had their origins in "hard" play. Assign independent research on any of the following:

- the Velcro fastener, George de Mestral
- sneakers, Charles Goodyear, Jr.
- the sandwich, John Montagu
- the hot air balloon, Jacques and Joseph Montgolfier
- the steam condenser, James Watt
- the aqualung (scuba), Jacques Cousteau

The ancient Greeks understood that we should have fun with our work and work at our play. Their word for education, *paideia*, was almost identical to their word for play, *paidia*!

When Life Is Not Fair

All the time-management skills in the world cannot overcome certain facts about our lives—a rough home situation, a physical or mental disability, shortage of skill, talent, or good looks. Middle schoolers viewing themselves with the hypercritical eyes of adolescence are acutely aware of their own advantages and disadvantages. "But you don't understand!" they cry. "Life's just not fair!"

Take some time to meet this real concern head on. Bring a large gift-wrapped package to class and explain that each of us comes into the world just like a package, a mysterious box of unknown personality, brains, and talents. Discuss with students the fact that we have no choice in our race, our sex, our family, our genetic makeup, our circumstances, or the century during which we live. Therefore, we deserve none of the credit for beauty, brains, a good home life, an athletic body, or a beautiful singing voice. The only thing in our power to manage is what happens after the package is opened. We are responsible in our own lives for what we do with what we have been given. That means we have two choices—to use our disadvantages as excuses, or to get busy and work hard, making the most of our advantages.

Now, open the gift box and pass it around the room. Students each pull out a strip of affirmation. Here are some sample messages:

- A tough situation will not defeat me. I will use it to strengthen me
- It is up to me to make the most of my talents and abilities.
- I will look for good things to happen to me, even if my path is rough.
- I will be an overcomer.
- I am responsible for what I do with what I have.

Take Time

One of the misconceptions of youth is that there will always be plenty of time. How often do we realize—a moment too late—that some opportunities pass our way just once, never to come again. All the regrets in the world cannot redeem time lost. It takes a thoughtful person to recognize those "once-in-a-lifetime" moments. With your students, make a list of opportunities we might miss if we are too busy pursuing our own goals. Here are a few examples:

- talking with a grandparent about the "olden" days.
- taking a younger brother on his first fishing trip.

- helping someone in an emergency.
- rebuilding a damaged relationship before it is too late.

Send students out armed with journals to participate in a once-in-a-lifetime event. Direct students to record their thoughts and respond to these questions: What took place here that may never happen again? What did you learn? Why is this event significant in someone's life? Did this situation create a special bond between you and the other people involved?

Achieving Goals

Youthful Successes

Most students view getting an education as a l-o-n-g term goal. But success might come sooner than they think. Motivate learning with this list of young achievers. Assign biography reading, independent research, or cooperative projects to discover why these individuals experienced success at such young ages.

- Mary Anning at 12 discovered the first ichthyosaur fossil.
- Louis Braille at 16 developed a method for the blind to read.
- Joan of Arc at 17 led the French army.
- Galileo at 18 developed the principle of the pendulum.
- George Washington at 19 was appointed adjutant general, at 21 was sent to negotiate with the French.
- Lafayette at 20 was made a general in the French army.
- Martin Luther at 29 began the Reformation that changed church history.
- Alexander the Great at 33 ruled the known world.
- William Shakespeare at 36 wrote masterpieces.

Making Corrections

Staying on Course

Your students will be fascinated to learn that the rocket which flew the *Apollo* mission to the moon in 1969 was off course 90 percent of the time. To remedy this problem, NASA monitored the flight continually and ordered thousands of minor adjustments throughout the mission.

We should follow NASA's example in scrutinizing our own course of action. Teach students to use those final minutes at bedtime before falling asleep as a time of evaluation. We need to ask ourselves about the goals for the day. Did we meet them? What hurt our progress? What helped? Bedtime can also be a good time to rehearse mentally the challenges of the coming day. What tasks do we need to accomplish? Which are the most important ones? Which could be done later? Like NASA, we may need to correct our course along the way, but the only thing that matters is landing in the right place.

Learning From Failure
The Open Door

A wise man once said, "Mistakes are the doors of discovery." To help students understand the meaning of this saying, divide them into groups to list the positive and negative outcomes of failure. Their lists may look similar to these:

Negative: Making a mistake is discouraging; it causes people to give up; it makes people angry or embarrassed.

Positive: You usually learn a lesson when you make a mistake; it makes success more meaningful; it helps you understand other people's failures.

Next, hand out small pieces of paper and have each student write down a mistake he or she made in the past and the specific lessons learned from it. Students then fold the notes into tiny squares and tape them to the classroom door frame. Remind them as they leave the room through this door that no mistake is ever wasted, as long as we use it to enter the door of discovery. Afterwards, remove the squares and dispose of them to keep students' responses private.

Coping With Failure
Character Studies

A skilled novelist can create characters who are so real, they leap off the printed page and into our hearts. We like these fictional people because we can identify with them. They have strength, but they also have lovable faults and failures, just as real human beings do. The writer knows that his/her readers like a character who struggles to behave much more than one who behaves all the time. With your students, make a list of favorite book personalities who fit this description. Identify the lovable weaknesses in each.

Tom Sawyer (*The Adventures of Tom Sawyer*)—sneaky, gets others to do his work
Willy Wonka (*Charlie and the Chocolate Factory*)—impatient, unforgiving
Wilbur (*Charlotte's Web*)—lazy, weepy
Laura Ingalls (*Little House on the Prairie*)—sometimes jealous of older sister, quick-tempered
Jesse (*Bridge to Terabithia*)—artsy loner
Winnie the Pooh (*Winnie the Pooh*)—enjoys food too much, makes up weird songs

Next, apply this understanding of human nature to our own lives Rather than ruining relationships, our failures and daily struggles often serve to bind us closer together. After all, who could stand having a friend who was always perfect? Will Rogers, an American entertainer of the 1930s, put it this way: "It's great to be great, but it's greater to be human." Failure is painful, but it helps keep us humble.

| Grand Finale Skit |

Time Management Saves the Day

This wrap-up skit, in the style of an old-fashioned melodrama, can be handled two ways. Divide the entire class into eight groups, or ask eight individual students to come to the front of the room. Assign each group or individual a sound effect to make when a key word appears in the script. If your class really gets into this, challenge them to write more sound-effect scripts of their own, working in as many time management principles as possible.

Key Words	Sounds to Make
Sweet Sue	"a-h-h-h-h-h"
Muddy Puddle Middle School	"slop-slop-slop"
Mr. Hardheart	"g-r-r-r-r"
pop quiz	"pop"
notes	"scribble-scribble-scribble"
report card	"o-o-o-h-h-h"
basketball team	"dribble-dribble-dribble"
time management	"tick-tick-tick-tick-tick"

The Story

Once there was a lovely lady named Sweet Sue.... who went to Muddy Puddle Middle School.... Now Sweet Sue.... tried her best to do well at Muddy Puddle Middle...., but she had a really tough social studies teacher, Mr. Hardheart.... Mr. Hardheart.... gave lots of pop quizzes.... and Sweet Sue.... and the other students at Muddly Puddle Middle.... took pages and pages of notes....

No mater how long she studied her notes...., Sweet Sue.... never made higher than a D on her report card.... Finally, Mr. Hardheart.... put his foot down. "Sweet Sue, ... if you do not take better notes.... and pass my pop quizzes...., I will have to take you off the basketball team.... for Muddy Puddle Middle...."

Poor Sweet Sue.... did not know what to do. Luckily, a guy named Smart Bart offered to help. "You are not dumb, Sweet Sue...." said Bart. "You just need to learn about time management.... Then you will pass those pop quizzes.... and keep your spot on the basketball team...."

So Sweet Sue.... and Smart Bart worked together every afternoon in the library of Muddy Puddle Middle.... They studied how to take notes.... and how to keep an assignment book. They studied in small chunks and followed other principles of time management....At last Bart felt like Sweet Sue... was ready.

"Wait until Mr. Hardheart.... sees your next pop quiz...," Bart said.

Sure enough, Sweet Sue.... did so well, she came up to a B on her report card.... and she kept her spot on the basketball team.... of Muddy Puddle Middle.... But that was not all!

"Just think, Bart," sighed Sweet Sue.... "If it were not for time management...., I never would have gotten to know what a wonderful guy you are!"

Time Management Olympics

For an end-of-the-year review, plan a Time Management Olympics. Ask questions about the organizational skills covered during the year and keep track of students' scores. The fun comes in presenting the prizes. Award the top point-getters with any of the following:

- a roll of toilet paper for making l-o-n-g lists!
- a light bulb to help with "light bulb" ideas.
- a leaf-sized trash bag for big cleanup jobs.
- cotton balls for blocking out noise during study time.
- a Band-aid to heal mistakes.
- a battery for extra energy.
- a pair of scissors to cut big jobs down to size.

Letter to Students

A Timely Send-Off

Use the letter below to remind your students of the importance of spending time on the best things:

Dear_____

At this moment we stand together, you and I, on one of life's busy corners. Behind are the long lazy days of childhood, where time never seems to go fast enough. Stretched out in front of us are the exciting, filled-to-overflowing times of adulthood. As you prepare to turn the corner and enter into that busy new world, I send you off with one last message.

Very quickly now, the days ahead will fill up with lessons, and meetings, and dances, and games, and plans, and jobs, and responsibilities. But always remember . . .

Take time to laugh. It will lighten your load.
Take time to love. It makes life worth living.
Take time to read. It is the source of wisdom.
Take time to dream. It can change the world.

May you *live* the days of your life!

Student Reproducibles—Chapter Seven

Put Yourself in the Picture!—Examines success cycle; answers will vary. Provide posterboard, scissors, and glue for students to make motivational picture frames.

Cape Canaveral Countdown—Changing habits progress chart. Extend by assigning written evaluations on students' 21-day efforts to change behavior.

All-Right People, All-Wrong Thinking—Perfectionism; answers: 1. D, 2. B, 3. E, 4. A, 5. C.

Who Said That?—Review of time management principles; answers: 1. B, 2. G, 3. H, 4. E, 5. A, 6. D, 7. C, 8. F. Extend by challenging students to come up with fictitious time management quotes from other famous people.

Put Yourself in the Picture!

Success Cycle

Look at the picture frame below. Where does the sentence start and where does it stop? No matter which phrase you begin with, the sentence makes sense.

THE BETTER I DO, THE MORE WORTHWHILE I FEEL.
THE MORE WORTHWHILE I FEEL, THE BETTER I DO.

These two sentences show how success is a cycle that goes around and around. When we do well in something, it makes us feel good, which in turn helps us to do better, which makes us feel good again, which ....

In the space below, write how the Success Cycle has worked for you: _____

_____

_____

Now put yourself in the picture! Cut out the frame, color it and mount it on cardboard. Glue a wallet-sized photo of yourself in the center. Keep your frame on your desk at home to help you remember that the Success Cycle begins with YOU!

Cape Canaveral Countdown

Changing Habits

Cape Canaveral, Florida, is NASA's space flight launching center. Most U.S. missions have been launched from the cape, including Neil Armstrong's flight to the moon in 1969 and the first reusable space shuttle in 1989. The rocket complex stays busy even between flights. It requires around-the-clock effort to be ready for the next liftoff.

Changing habits requires constant work, too. Scientists who study human behavior say that it takes 21 consecutive days to make or break a new habit, 21 days in a row before the change becomes automatic. Do you have a behavior you would like to change? Make it a point to practice the new behavior for 21 days. If you skip a day, you will have to start all the way back at Day One! Use this chart to keep track of your progress.

The habit I want to change is:

_____

_____

_____

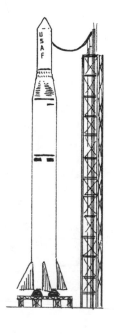

1	2	3
4	5	6
7	8	9
10	11	12
13	14	15
16	17	18
19	20	21

Name_____

All-Right People, All-Wrong Thinking

Maintaining Perspective

Once you learn to be a good time manager, you start to get used to success. And success is great—if you keep the proper perspective. Sometimes you get so used to success, you cannot settle for anything else. The students below have learned to do all the right things, but they have all the wrong thinking. Label each quotation with the letter of the matching problem.

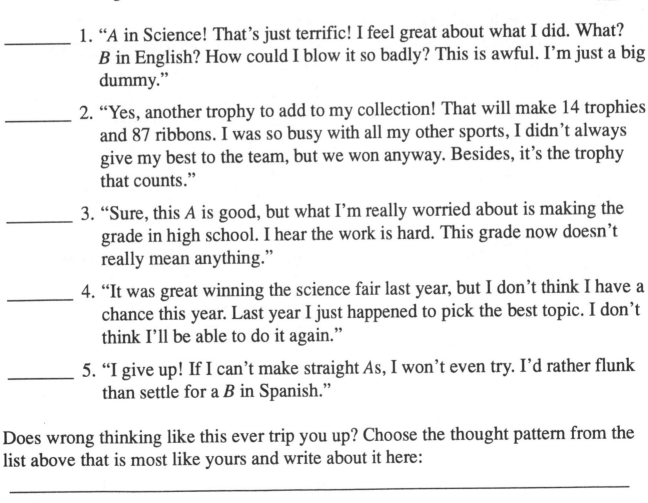

A. Living in the Past
B. Quantity, Not Quality
C. All or Nothing
D. Mood Swinging
E. Focusing on the Future

_____ 1. "*A* in Science! That's just terrific! I feel great about what I did. What? *B* in English? How could I blow it so badly? This is awful. I'm just a big dummy."

_____ 2. "Yes, another trophy to add to my collection! That will make 14 trophies and 87 ribbons. I was so busy with all my other sports, I didn't always give my best to the team, but we won anyway. Besides, it's the trophy that counts."

_____ 3. "Sure, this *A* is good, but what I'm really worried about is making the grade in high school. I hear the work is hard. This grade now doesn't really mean anything."

_____ 4. "It was great winning the science fair last year, but I don't think I have a chance this year. Last year I just happened to pick the best topic. I don't think I'll be able to do it again."

_____ 5. "I give up! If I can't make straight *A*s, I won't even try. I'd rather flunk than settle for a *B* in Spanish."

Does wrong thinking like this ever trip you up? Choose the thought pattern from the list above that is most like yours and write about it here:

_____

_____

Who Said That?

Reviewing Principles

The quotations below are pure fiction, but see if you can match the famous people with the words they might have said about their successes. Write a letter in each blank.

A.	Louis Braille	E.	Clara Barton
B.	Sally Ride	F.	George Washington Carver
C.	Leonardo da Vinci	G.	John James Audubon
D.	Daniel Boone	H.	Mark Twain

_____1. "I had to take many difficult courses to qualify for the space program. The secret to my success was always doing the hardest things first, while I was fresh."

_____2. "I was lucky! My work was extremely difficult, but I enjoyed it so much, it felt like play. Who wouldn't want to watch and draw birds all day?"

_____3. "Believe it or not, the hardest thing about being a writer is sitting still long enough to get the job done. I had to find my best time of day to work and stick with it to finish *The Adventures of Huckleberry Finn*."

_____4. "I am so glad I learned to make minutes count! During the Civil War, my nurses rolled bandages even when they sat down to take a break!"

_____5. "The world just saw me as a handicapped boy, but I saw my blindness as an opportunity to develop a reading system for the blind."

_____6. "I admit I was a failure when it came to building a life in one place. But I put my wanderlust to work and marked a trail through North Carolina, Virginia, Tennessee, and Kentucky for other settlers to use."

_____7. "My best secret is my notebook. I kept it with me at all times, to write down ideas and make sketches. The different faces from my painting *The Last Supper* came straight from my notes!"

_____8. "I had an enormous mental block about how to use the peanut plant. My brain was just blank. But I took a little time off and relaxed, and then ideas started coming by the dozens! I eventually came up with over 300 uses for the peanut."